Gino Moretto

THE SHROUD
A GUIDE

English Translation by Alan Neame

Paulist Press
New York, N.Y. • Mahwah, N.J.

Gino Moretto was born at Villadose, Rovigo, Italy, in 1924. Turinese by adoption since 1957, he has for many years been interested in the Problem of the Shroud.
In 1987, Professor Pierluigi Baima Bollone, Director of the International Centre of Sindonology of Turin, appointed him secretary to the Guild, numbering more than two thousand Corresponding Members all over the world. He is also editorial secretary of the review Sindon.
In this book, illustrated with more than 160 photographs, very rare ones, some never published before, his aim has been to answer the many questions put to him by scores of visitors to the Museum of the Shroud, where he is always ready to meet you... but by appointment, please!

Front cover:
The Holy Face, taken from the Shroud of Turin
by Mario Caffaro Rore

Copyright © Editrice Elle Di Ci, 1996 - 10096 Leumann, Torino, Italy

English Language Copyright © ST PAULS, 1998

Published in the United States by
Paulist Press
997 Macarthur Boulevard
Mahwah, New Jersey 07430

Library of Congress Cataloging-in-Publication Data

Moretto, Gino, 1924-
   [Sindone. English]
     The Shroud: a guide / Gino Moretto: English translation by
Alan Neame.
     p. cm.
   Includes bibliographical references.
   ISBN 0-8091-3886-7 (alk. paper)
   1. Holy Shroud, I. Title
BT587.S4M6713 1999
232.96'6–dc21

99-11635
CIP

Printed in Italy

Table of Contents

Foreword	5
To the reader	6
Acknowledgements	6
A guide to reading the Shroud	7

How where when — 13

The Shroud of Turin	15
The Gospels and History are silent for the first thirteen centuries	17
The Shroud reaches first France and then Italy	17
The imprints	18
First at Lirey, then at Chambéry	19
The Shroud after the fire of 1532	20
From Chambéry to Turin	21
Turin – The Chapel of the Shroud	22
The Exposition of 1898	24
The first photograph of the Shroud	25
The Exposition of 1931	27
The Exposition of 1933	31
1939-1946 – The Shroud at Montevergine	32
The official photographs of 1969	33
1973 – First televised Exposition and first samples taken from the cloth of the Shroud	34
1978 – Exposition for 43 days. Direct examination for 120 hours	35
1980 – The pilgrimage to Turin of Pope John Paul II	37
1983 – From the House of Savoy to the Holy See	37
1992 – Inspection of the Shroud to ensure its better conservation	38
1993 – The Shroud is temporarily moved	40

Scientific Research — 41

1969 – For the first time the Shroud examined by scientific experts	43
Studies in the origin of the imprints	44
1976 – Reports of the Experts	46
Study and research	47
The Shroud and information technology	51
Is the Shroud the iconographical model for ancient pictures of Jesus?	52
1988 – Examination of samples from the Shroud by Radio-Carbon	54
The Shroud of Turin and the Napkin of Oviedo	56
What about other shrouds?	57
Can the Man of the Shroud be identified?	58

On the medical examiner's table — 59

Imprint of the forehead	60
The wound in the chest	62
The forearms and the hands	64
The nape and upper part of the back	66
The blood-flow across the back	68
Imprint of the feet from behind	70
Conclusion	72

Judgements and decisions of the ecclesiastical authorities — 73

Pius XI and Pius XII	74
John XXIII and Paul VI	75
John Paul II	76
Cardinal Giovanni Saldarini	76
Announcement on Expositions of the Shroud in the years 1998 and 2000	77
Statement on experiments concerning the Holy Shroud	77
The Confraternity of the Most Holy Shroud. The International Centre of Sindonology of Turin	78
The Museum of the Shroud	79

To the reader

Ever more often, even if for conflicting reasons, we are reminded of the existence of a unique document called THE SHROUD, which has been preserved in Turin Cathedral for more than four hundred years.

We have each of us – with the help of the media – formed our personal idea about this object, which has been described as a challenge to Science, and there is no doubt that the Shroud is a challenge to the human mind, even the most sceptical.

The purpose of this book – far from purely scientific considerations but not ignoring these – is to assist the pilgrim, given the imminent Exposition, in 'reading' the image on the Shroud in the light of whatever solid knowledge about it has as yet been acquired, in knowing its 'history' and, as far as maybe, in understanding the imprints venerated on this piece of linen.

The Shroud is certainly the most studied, most discussed, whether accepted or rejected, of objects, ever fascinating even though still, or indeed because still, mysterious. Is the Man of the Shroud the Man of the Gospels? This is the most disturbing of the questions it raises. What can we answer? I do not know whether Jesus, after death, was laid in this piece of cloth; I do not know how the image was formed on it; but I do know that this image bears a very close relationship to the gospel description of the passion, crucifixion and death of Jesus: a sacred document described by Pope John Paul II as 'the most splendid relic of the Passion and the resurrection' (*Osservatore Romano*, April 21-22, 1980, p.2).

Gentle reader, read indulgently what I in my simplicity have written and illustrated in this book. It is intended, as I said before, just to be a modest help to 'reading', without prejudice – the exhibit before which even Science stands bewildered.

THE AUTHOR

Acknowledgement

I have only been able to complete this work thanks to the help of many friends.

First of all the photographer Aldo Guerreschi, owner of Studio SCOFFONE, Turin, for having provided me with the excellent photographs developed from Enrie's original plates which he has optimised to an amazing degree, and also for those photographs which he took himself.

For the advance reading of the text, my thanks to Professor Don Giuseppe Ghiberti and the members of the Steering Committee of the Centro Internazionale di Sindonologia di Torino (International Centre of Sindonology, Turin), of which for the past eight years or so I have held the office of Secretary.

I cannot forget my friends Mario Moroni, Ezio Dutto, Giovanni Battista Judica Cordiglia and the architect Maurizio Momo for the photographical material with which only they could have provided me.

Special thanks to the artist Mario Caffaro Rore for permission to reproduce some of his paintings adorning this book.

The image of the human figure must be 'read' as though reflected in a mirror:
what you see on the figure's right is actually on its left, and vice-versa.
The imprint of the human body is a *negative* image, the body-marks and the bleeding wounds are in *positive*.

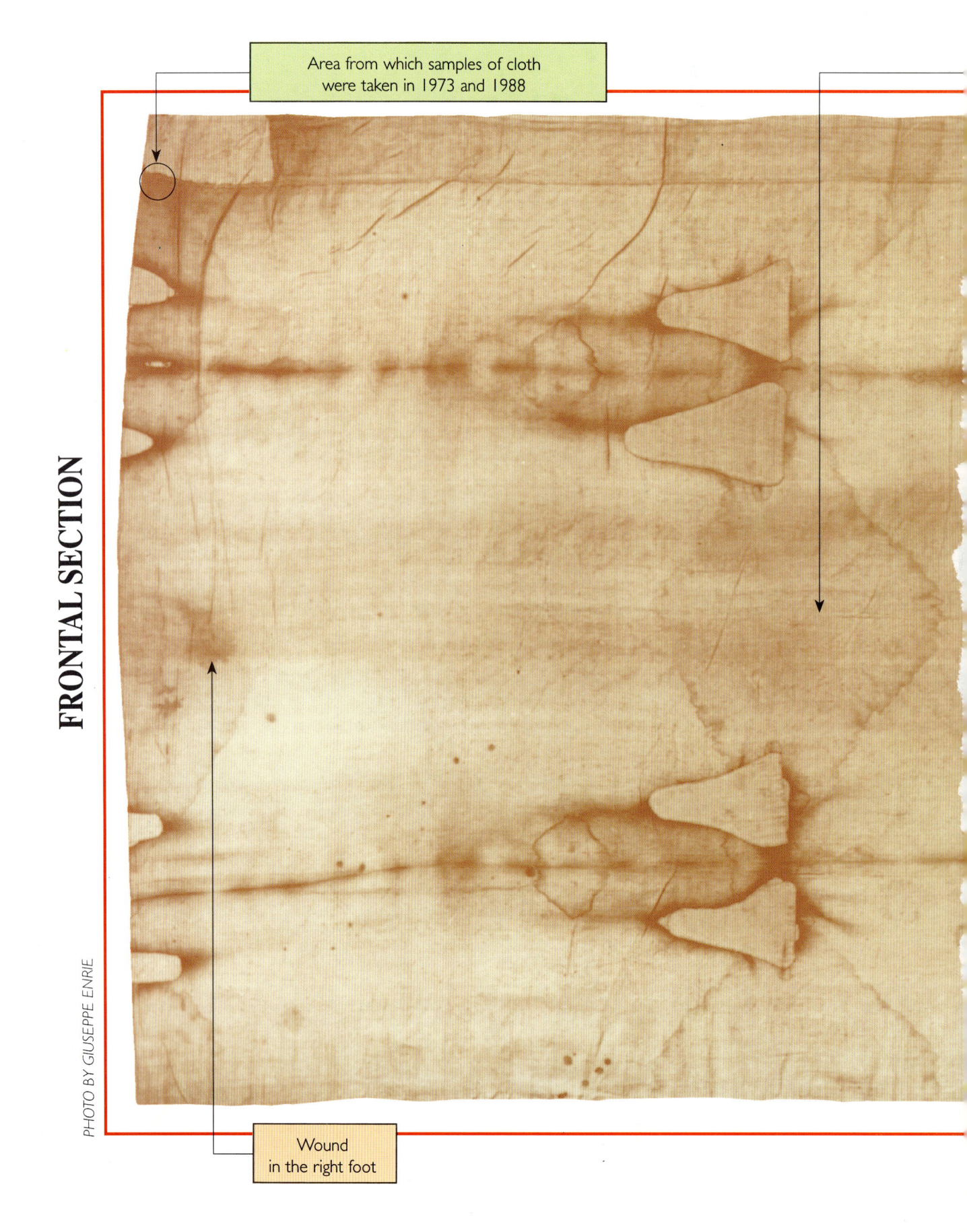

Area from which samples of cloth were taken in 1973 and 1988

FRONTAL SECTION

PHOTO BY GIUSEPPE ENRIE

Wound in the right foot

The Holy Shroud in photographic *positive*, i.e. as it looks to the eye of the observer.

A guide to rea

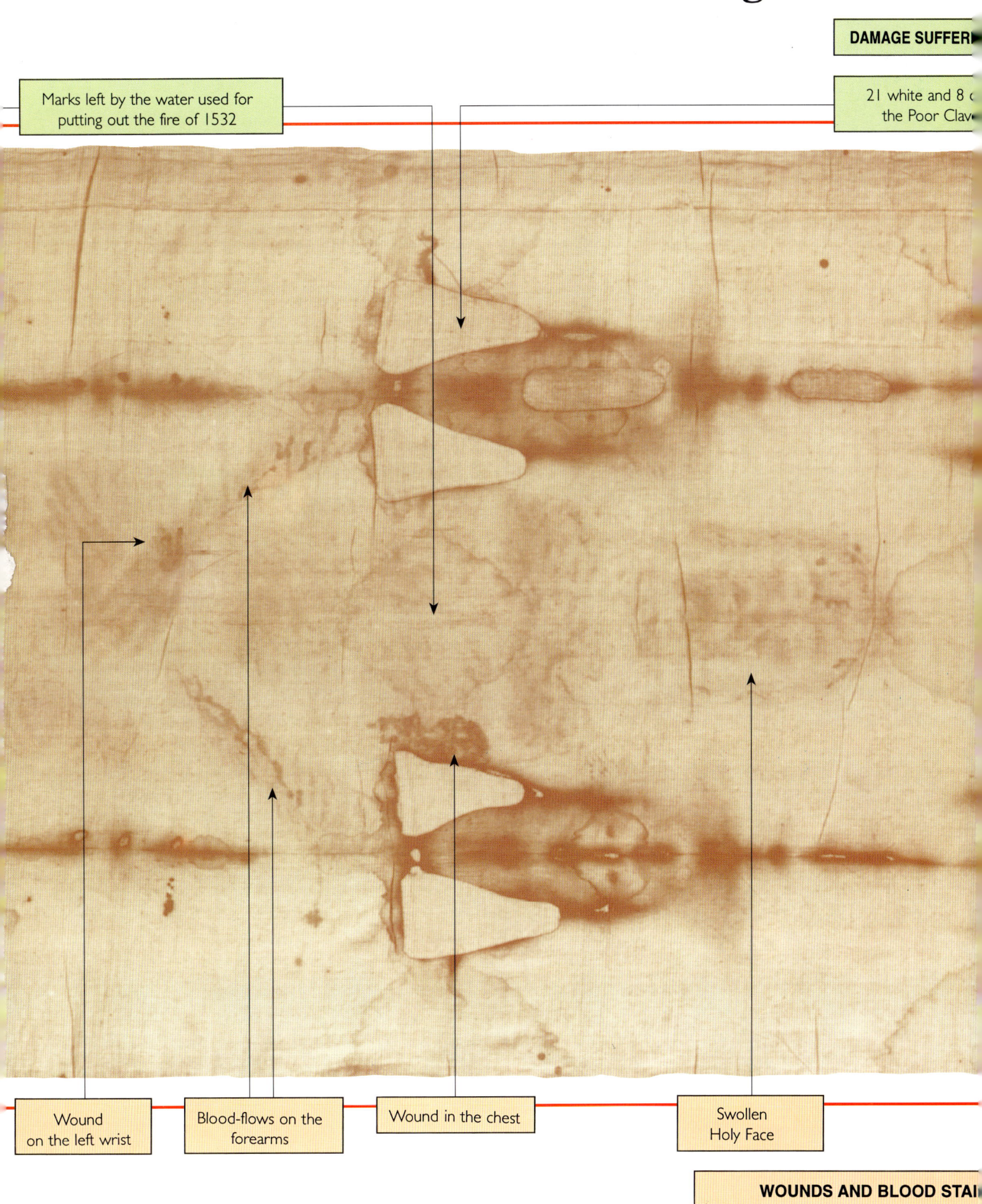

DAMAGE SUFFER

Marks left by the water used for putting out the fire of 1532

21 white and 8 o
the Poor Clav

| Wound on the left wrist | Blood-flows on the forearms | Wound in the chest | Swollen Holy Face |

WOUNDS AND BLOOD STAI

Foreword
by Cardinal Giovanni Saldarini

In Turin four hundred and twenty years ago there appeared a mysterious object that has become more and more famous with the passing of the years. The origin of the mystery lay with its being called the Sindon (a Greek word meaning Shroud) and was prolonged by the image it bore imprinted on it, reaching its apogee once people began trying to grasp the meaning of that image.

The word *Sindon* comes from the Gospels, where they tell of the linens in which Jesus was buried; the image represents a man who has died after undergoing the torments of crucifixion; the meaning of the image lies in the reasons why this man was crucified.

Why was he crucified? What were his feelings as he hung dying on the cross? Death in itself is ever an impenetrable mystery; it is especially so where this man's fate is concerned, who gazes serenely at us from his winding-sheet.

Our first ray of light comes from a mysterious book: the Gospel written by Mark, Matthew, Luke and John in four differing yet very similar versions. The gospel narrative and the Shroud image seem like reflections of one another.

But how has that image been formed and why does it offer so impressive a reminder of that Man, recollections about whom seem otherwise to be confined to the gospel narrative alone?

Questions press in, one after another, and our answers are ever very uncertain, Yet uncertainties cannot obscure the radiance of the known facts, which cannot but influence our lives. The Shroud speaks of Jesus, of his death, of his love for human beings, each and every one of us. As we look at the Shroud we cannot fail to think of our own sins, which were the cause of so much suffering but could not manage to quench so great a love.

One might then say there is no need to know a great deal about the Shroud. True, the Shroud speaks to the life of each of us, even to those who have no specialist knowledge. Yet, within us, we feel a need to know, and this is no superficial curiosity but, rather, instinctive love. That is why so many people ponder over the Shroud and why, the more they know, the more they feel impelled to study it deeper: on the level of scientific problems as also that of its effect on our lives.

The author of this book has spent many years immersed in the mysteries of which he writes and for which he has sought answers. Initially he did this for himself, then with the aim of helping many others. Thus this guidebook was born, offering an approach to the Shroud. The text is admirably spare in style. The essential facts are set out briefly, backed by a truly exceptional dossier of photographs.

You may skim through this guide, reading it straight through; alternatively you may adopt a more measured approach, taking it stage by stage. It is so excitingly laid out that most readers will read it in one go. But afterwards they will want to enjoy going back over the details. If then this reading is crowned with a pilgrimage to the Holy Shroud during the Expositions now imminent in 1998 and 2000, the fruit of the author's labours will be enjoyed in its totality.

The information contained in these pages will interest those who have a living faith in the Lord Jesus, and also those who follow another road. But all will have cause to rejoice when they see what effect a message such as this can have on the life of any individual: the challenge put to us by the ineffable history of this linen Sheet.

✠ GIOVANNI CARD. SALDARINI
Archbishop of Turin

DORSAL SECTION

...g the Shroud

...E SACRED CLOTH

...atches put on by
...mbéry in 1534.

Burns and holes left by an earlier fire than that of 1532

Drops and trickles of blood from the nape of the neck

Abrasion on the shoulder-blade and shoulder

Blood-flow on the loins

THE MAN OF THE SHROUD

Longitudinal lines of charring from the fire of 1532

DORSAL SECTION

Scourge blows

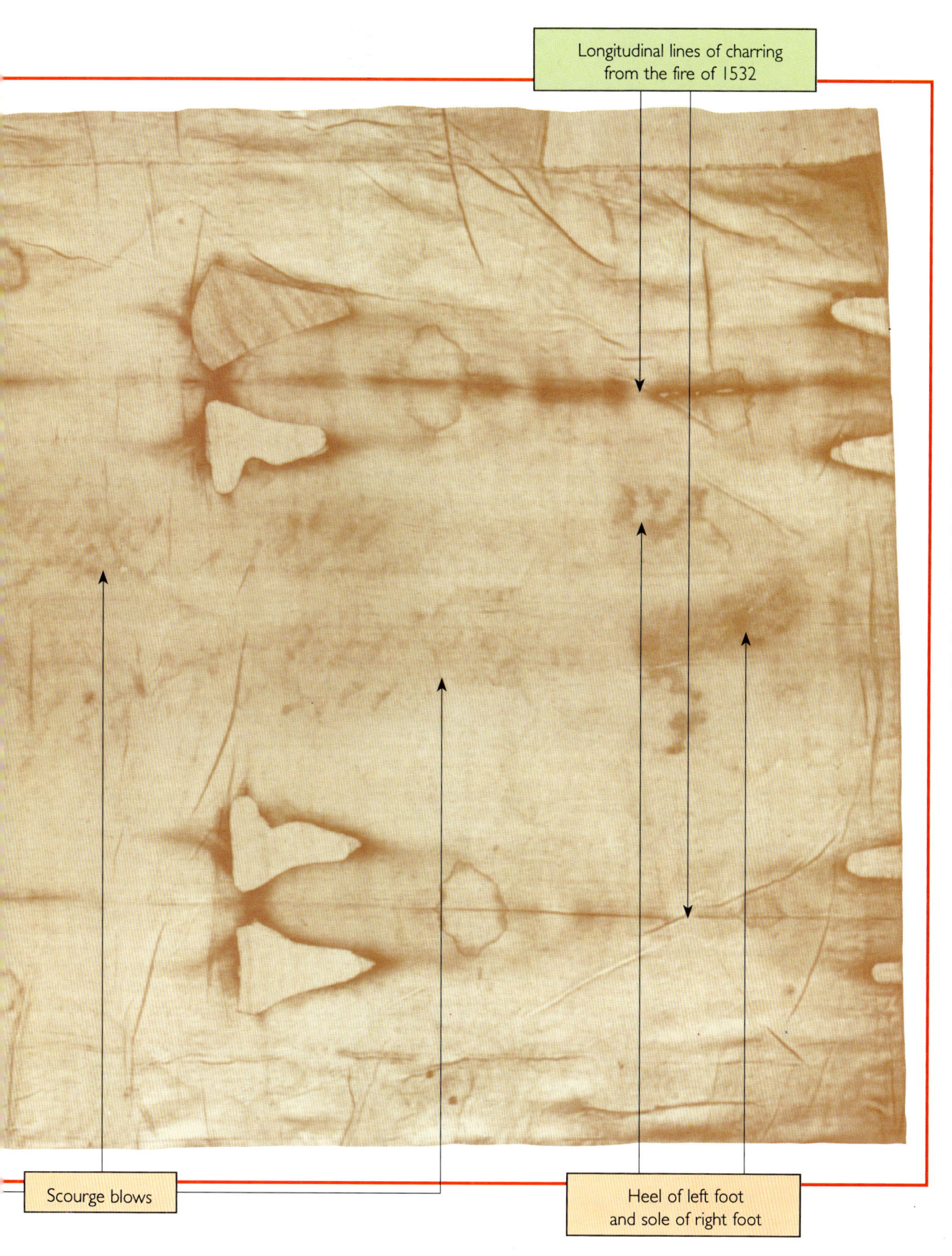

Heel of left foot and sole of right foot

FRONTAL SECTION

On these two pages the frontal and dorsal sections of the Shroud are shown separately, vertically and in photographic negative to make the human figure easier to read.

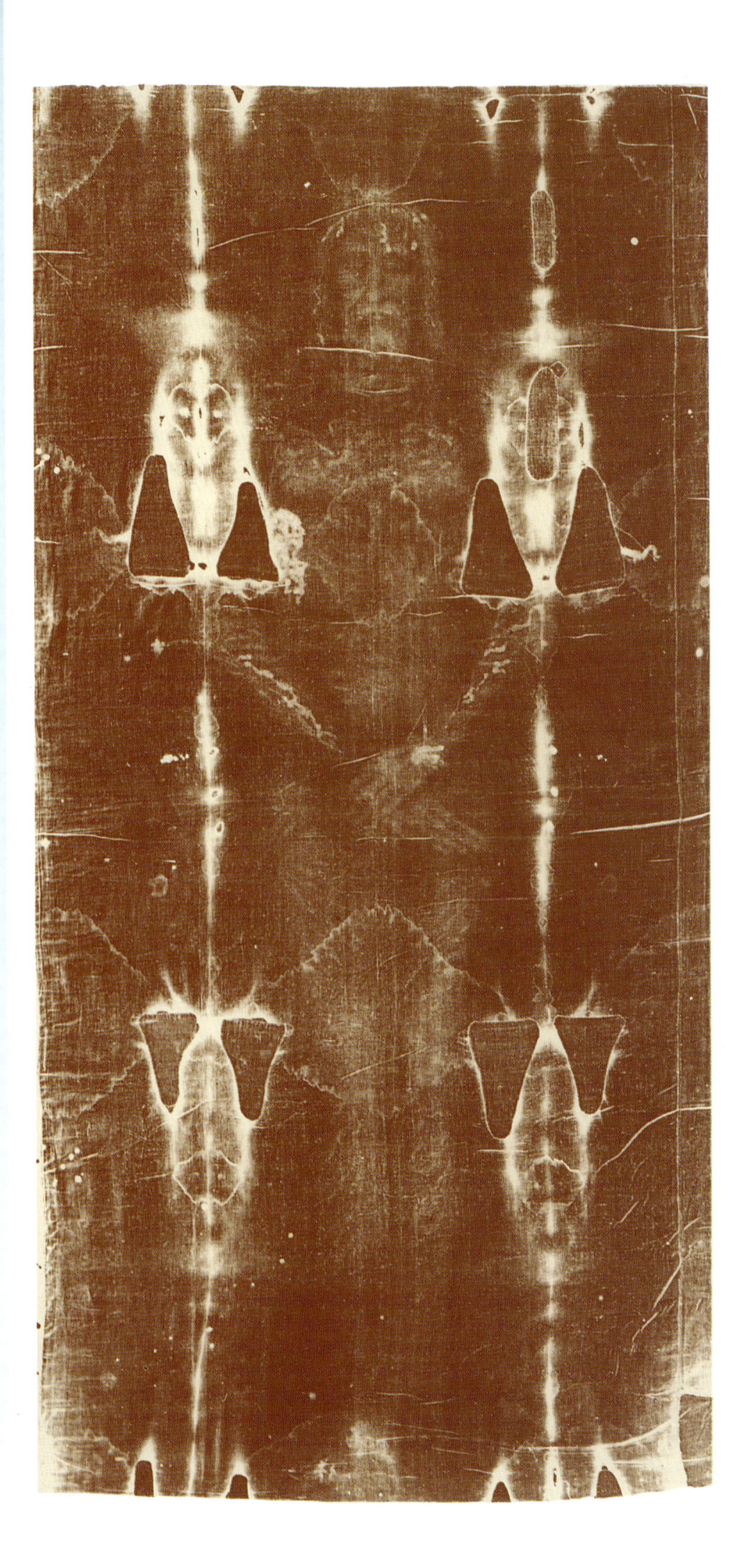

HOW
WHERE
WHEN

*In this book I did not set out to present
a mere collection of photographs, fascinating though these might be,
but to use the persuasive language of the image
to make it easier to understand the mysterious imprint,
acheropita (not made by human hand) that the Holy Shroud displays to us.*

Drawing by MARIO CAFFARO RORE

The Shroud of Turin

What it is?

It is a linen sheet of herringbone weave, 436 cm long and 110 cm wide, including a longitudinal strip of about 8 cm.

On one side only of the cloth can be seen the frontal and dorsal imprints of a man who has died after being crucified.

Ancient tradition identifies this Shroud – a document agreeing in every respect with the Passion, Crucifixion and Death of Jesus – as the one which is mentioned in the Gospels.

The Greek word *SINDON*, while having different meanings (*TUNIC, MANTLE, TABLECLOTH* &c.), generally means the *WINDING-SHEET* in which Jesus Christ was wrapped after his death.

The weave of the Shroud.

What the Gospels say

All four evangelists (Mk 15:42-47; Mt 27:57-61; Lk 23: 50-56 and Jn 19:38-42) relate how Jesus was placed in 'the new tomb nearby that Joseph of Arimathaea had had hewn out of the rock', and the first three evangelists say…

… after they had taken him down …

… they wrapped him in a sheet …

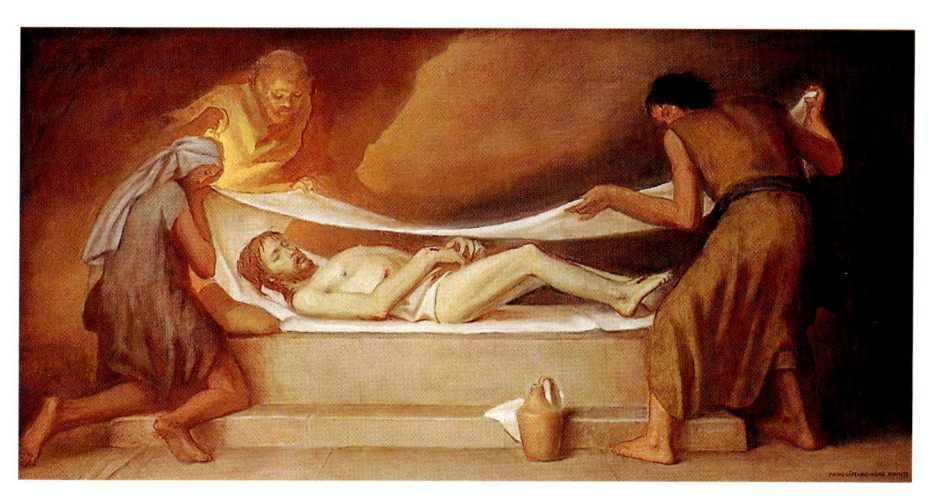

(Two paintings by M. Caffaro Rore)

Pope SYLVESTER I (314-335) at the Provincial Council of Terme di Traiano in Rome, ruled that the holy sacrifice of the Mass should be celebrated on a linen tablecloth consecrated by the Bishop, as though it were on the pure Shroud of Christ (*La Sindone e la Scienza*, Ed. Paoline 1978, p. 304).

... the stone had been rolled away
(Mk 16:4)

Photographs of two typical tombs with circular stones 20 centuries old but still to be seen in the western part of Jerusalem. One can see how the stone could be rolled across the entrance to the tomb. The tomb of Jesus was probably like this.

16

The Gospels and History are silent for the first thirteen centuries

The most frequent objections to the authenticity of the Shroud as a relic of Jesus are the silence of the Gospels over the recovery of his burial clothes, and the scarcity of historical documentation for the first thirteen centuries.

History, we know, doesn't record every event; sometimes it reveals facts little by little over long intervals.

More controversial is the silence of the Gospels.

First of all, however, the Shroud as document (existing today and always available to be checked) agrees in such minute details with the Gospel narrative of the passion and death of Jesus as to exclude casual coincidence; certain simple considerations also come to mind. The Beloved Disciple, who was an eye-witness to Christ's entire passion, is the one who, having said that Peter had entered the sepulchre first, adds: 'Then the other disciple went in too, who had been the first to arrive at the sepulchre, and he saw and believed' (Jn 20:8). Could he really have let himself be swayed by a puritanical formalism and have refused to touch the grave clothes, and not instead have lovingly gathered up these relics of his Divine Master in order to preserve them?

It is reasonable to suppose that, the 'legal impurity' of the Mosaic law being set aside, Christ's burial clothes were gathered up and jealously guarded, as certainly happened later in the iconoclastic period.

Even though not copious, historical references before the thirteenth century confirm the tradition of Christ's grave-clothes having been preserved and, although we cannot connect this with absolute documentary certainty with the Shroud of Turin, the references complement the facts established by scientific research on this piece of linen.

544
An extraordinary image 'not made by human hand' was preserved in Edessa (modern Urfa, Turkey). Many scholars identify this image with the Shroud, though it was kept folded in such a way as to display the face alone.

944
The image of Edessa was transferred to Constantinople. There it was unfurled full-length, allowing a complete view of the body.

1147
Louis VII, King of France, visited Constantinople and venerated the Shroud preserved there.

1204
When Constantinople was occupied by the Crusaders, many relics were dispersed. Written testimony from Crusaders exists, attesting that they have seen 'the Lord's Shroud'.

The Shroud reaches first France and then Italy

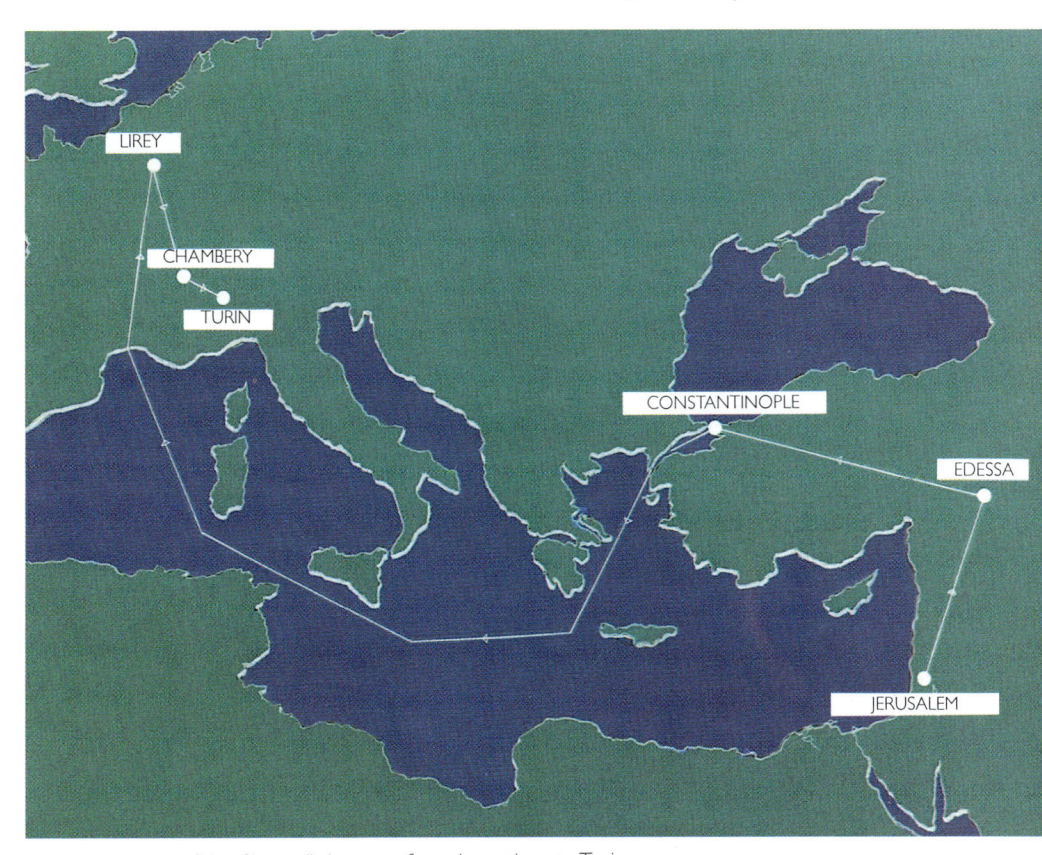

Possible course of the Shroud's journey from Jerusalem to Turin.

The imprints

Before the fires, the Shroud only bore the frontal and dorsal images of a human figure, with blood stains and bloody body-marks.

Damage caused by a fire earlier than that of Chambéry in 1532

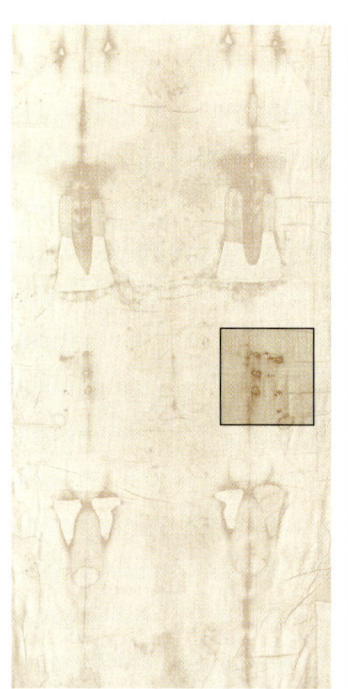

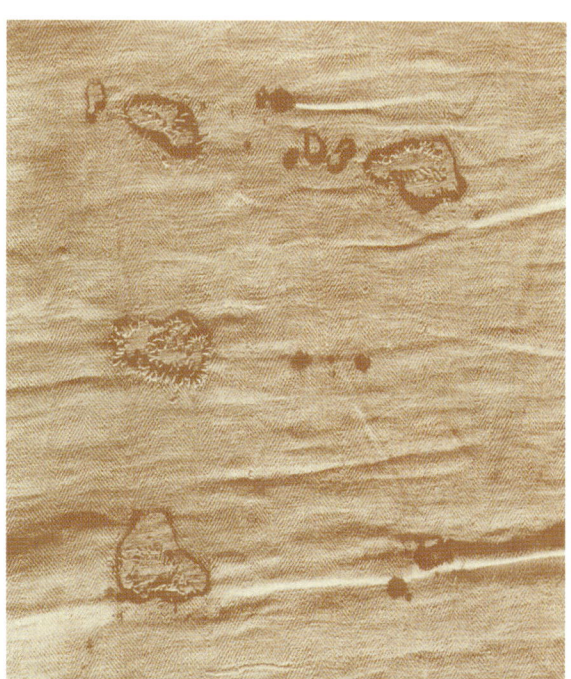

A series of burn-holes visible on the right-hand side of the dorsal section of the Shroud. Though more lightly, these are reflected in three other sectors of the Sacred Cloth.

Photo below:
This copy, dated 1516 and attributed to Albrecht Dürer (1471-1528), documents the fact that the Shroud had been through a fire at a time and in circumstances unknown, but certainly before the Chambéry fire of 1532; for it reproduces only the doubly mirror-image series of little burn-holes, visible in the Sacred Cloth today and clearly shown in the two photographs (left) here, whereas it does not show the burns and patching due to the fire of 1532.

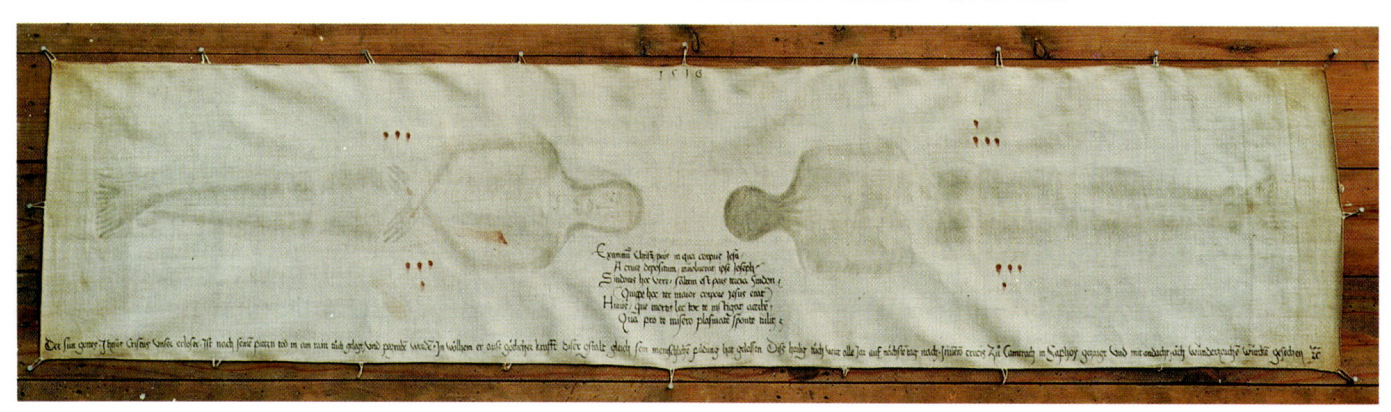

18

First at Lirey, then at Chambéry

1353 or thereabouts

The Shroud makes its appearance at Lirey, France, in the possession of Geoffroy de Charny. Henceforth the Shroud's presence in the West is rigorously documented.

Exterior of the Sainte-Chapelle

1453

The Shroud becomes the property of Louis, Duke of Savoy (see engraving), who transfers it to Chambéry, the capital of his domains.

1502

It is kept in a silver box which is placed in a niche cut into the choir-sacristy wall of the gothic-style Sainte-Chapelle, built for the purpose and the stone walls of which were lined with oak.
The church was called Sainte-Chapelle because – like the older one in Paris – it was designed to house relics of Christ's passion.

Interior of the Sainte-Chapelle

The niche (in those days protected by a grating) in which the Shroud was kept.

1532

During the night of December 3-4 fire broke out in the choir-sacristy of the Sainte-Chapelle.
One side of the silver box containing the folded Shroud became red hot due to the high temperature, and a drop of metal, melting from the lid, pierced through the various layers of the Sacred Cloth.

The Shroud after the fire of 1532

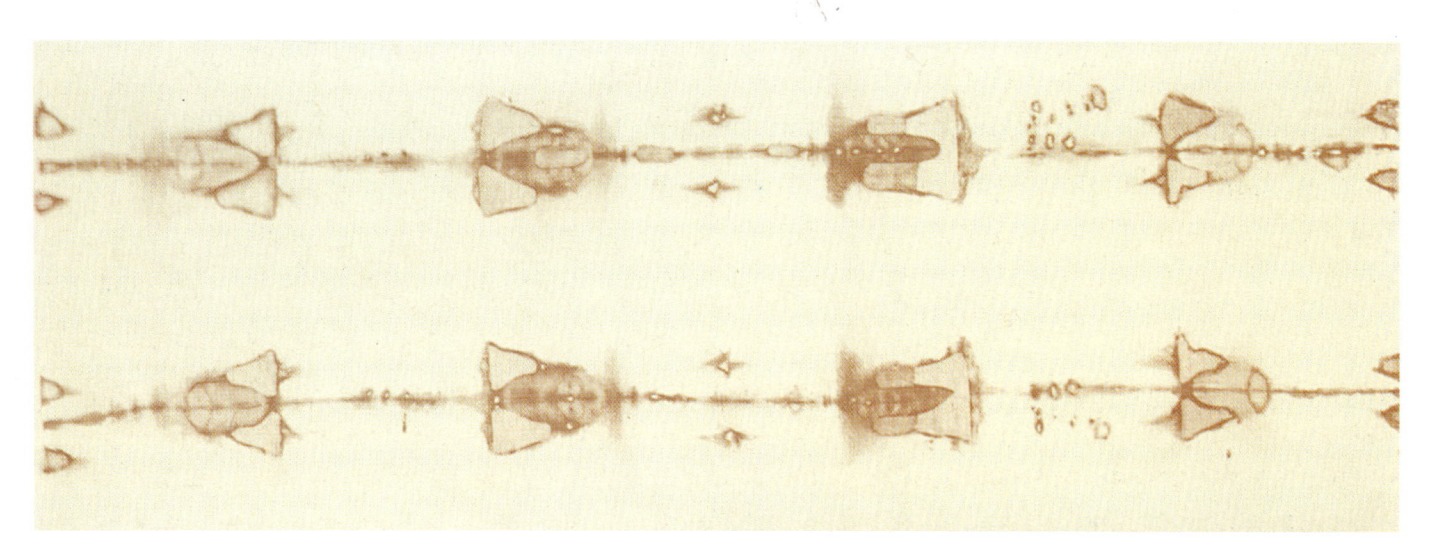

1534

From April 15 to May 2, the Poor Clares of Chambéry repair the parts burnt away by sewing on patches, still to be seen today.

Right: a threefold patch at the level of the upper part of the left arm (on the right as you look at the dorsal image of the Shroud).

The larger of the patches, U-shaped, is of white linen of smooth, fine weave; the material of the two extensions is also of finely woven linen but of a markedly darker, more amber, colour. Between the extensions darns can be seen to a frayed area, and these follow a line along the longitudinal axis of the burns.

The area shown in the photograph covers somewhat more than 60 sq. cm (28 x 22).

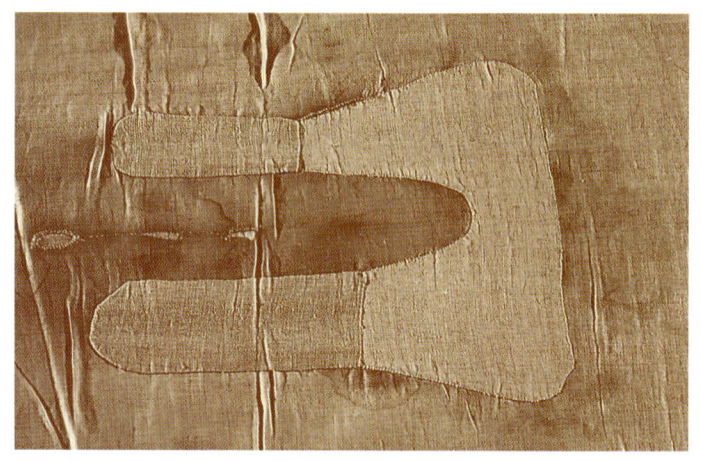

Photo by N. Pisano (by kind permission of the Archbishop of Turin).

Three macrophotographs of the damaged Shroud cloth

Left, traces of wax. Centre and right, burns and patching (Photo A Ghio, 1978).

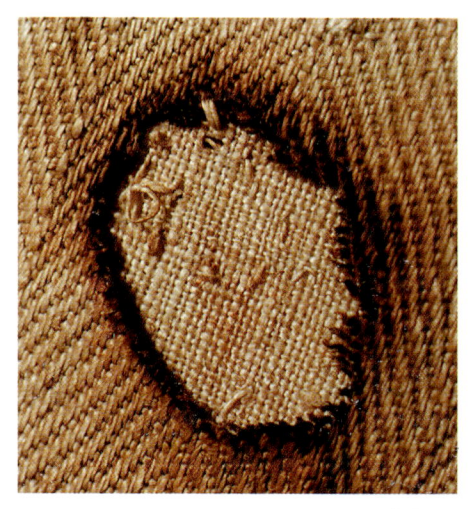

20

1578 – From Chambéry to Turin

On September 14, 1578, Duke Emmanuel Philibert transfers the Shroud to Turin, so as to shorten the tiring journey for Archbishop Charles Borromeo, the latter having resolved to betake himself on foot from Milan to Chambéry to venerate the Shroud in fulfilment of a vow made during the plague of 1576.

Stone placed at the entrance to the present church of Saint Laurence to commemorate the translation of the Shroud.

Casket used for transporting the Shroud from Chambéry to Turin (Museum of the Shroud, Turin).

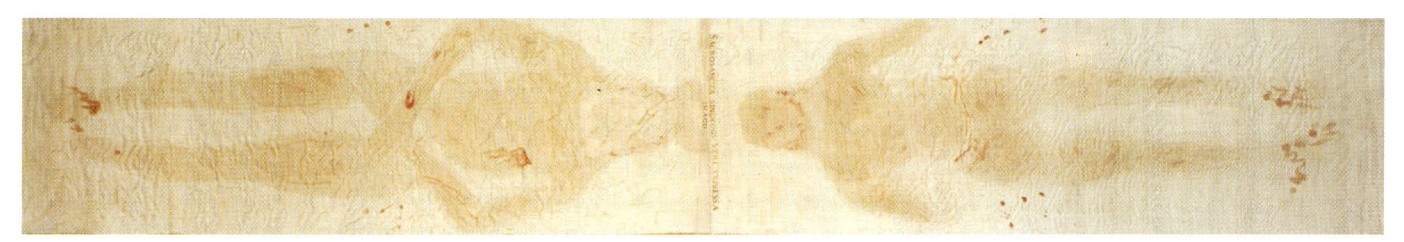

Copy of the Shroud given by Duke Emmanuel Philibert to Charles Borromeo when the Cardinal made his first pilgrimage to the Shroud in Turin. It was placed for some time, by order of the Duke himself, in direct contact with the Sacred Sheet.

It is datable most probably to the period before 1532 (the year of the Chambéry fire) by the absence on the painting of the patching done to the Shroud by the Poor Clares in 1534.

Turin – The Chapel of the Shroud
EXTERIOR

By his will, Duke Emmanuel Philibert ordained that the money to be collected for his burial was to be used for building the Chapel of the Shroud. Begun (in 1657) to the design of B. Quadri, building of the Chapel was continued (from 1667) and completed to the design of Guarino Guarini (1624-1683).

The Shroud was installed in it on June 1, 1694.

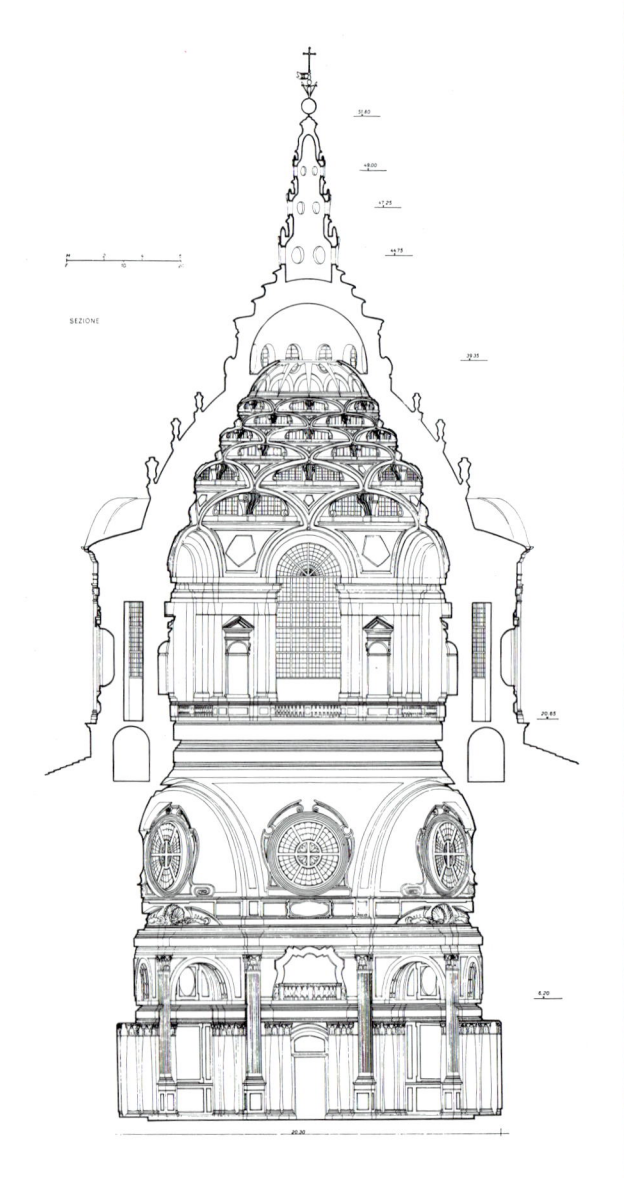

Above left: view of the cupola …

and above: a complete cross-section.

Left: The Cathedral of St John with the cupola of the Chapel of the Holy Shroud rising behind and above it.

22

Turin – The Chapel of the Shroud
INTERIOR

Cross-section of the Chapel in Guarini's original design.

Upper drum of the cupola.

The 16th century chased silver reliquary which contains the rolled-up Shroud today. It is kept in the ark standing on the pedestal above the altar and is protected by a grating which can only be opened with three keys. These are held by three different custodians; only when they are all present at the same time can the repository be unlocked.

Double-fronted altar, above which the Shroud has been kept since 1694 (Antonio Bertola, architect).

The Exposition of 1898

In 1898, Turin celebrated:

• the 50th anniversary of the Constitution granted by King Charles Albert in 1848;

• the 400th anniversary of the building of the present Cathedral (1491-1497), constructed on the site of three churches which together formed the old cathedral;

• the 3rd centenary of the founding of the Confraternity of the Most Holy Shroud and the Confraternity of St Roch;

• the 1500th anniversary of a Church Council held at Turin.

To mark and celebrate the convergence of all these civil and religious events, the First International Exhibition was held and with it an Exhibition of Sacred Art.

This was the occasion for holding the historic Exposition of the Holy Shroud, which took place from May 25 to June 2.

Above: interior of Turin Cathedral with the Holy Shroud exposed above the high altar.

Right: a souvenir card of the 1898 Exposition.

24

The first photograph of the Shroud

During the 1898 Exposition, the House of Savoy, owners of the relic, authorised the lawyer Secondo Pia, a devotee of the 'new art' of photography, to photograph the Holy Shroud for the first time ever.
He took two test photographs (21 x 27 cm) on May 25 and another two on May 28, when he also took the four official photographs (format 50 x 60 cm): in all, eight full-length photographs with different time exposures. The result was amazing, even though the photographs had been taken through the glass of the frame and the latter was a few centimetres shorter than the Sacred Cloth itself.

Above: the four test photographs:
1. strictly speaking the first ever, with one-minute exposure; 2. with two-minute exposure; 3. with three-minute exposure, and 4. with five-minute exposure.

Fav left: the lawyer Secondo Pia.

Left: the camera with which he photographed the Holy Shroud (Museum of the Shroud, Turin).

PHOTOGRAPHY REVEALS THAT THE SHROUD IMAGE BEHAVES AS A NATURAL NEGATIVE

Negative of the original Plate 4 of Pia's test photographs. It is reproduced at 65% of its actual size.

Beneath the unfolded Shroud, the altar on which it stands is also in the picture, but whereas the altar is in *photographic negative* (first stage of reproduction), the image on the Shroud can be seen in *photographic positive* (which no one could have foreseen), showing that the human figure on the cloth is inexplicably printed in *natural negative*.

This road leads us into the heart of a mystery which has been indecipherable for centuries!

Right: here you can see what the altar and Shroud looked like to the naked eye.

The Exposition of 1931

To crown the festivities in honour of the marriage of the Prince of Piedmont, Umberto of Savoy, and Priness Maria Josè of Belgium – celebrated on January 8, 1930 – a memorable Exposition of the Holy Shroud was held from May 3 to May 24, 1931.

Face and obverse of the medal struck to commemorate the occasion.

The altar prepared for the occasion, designed by G. Casanova.

The Shroud exposed in Turin Cathedral.

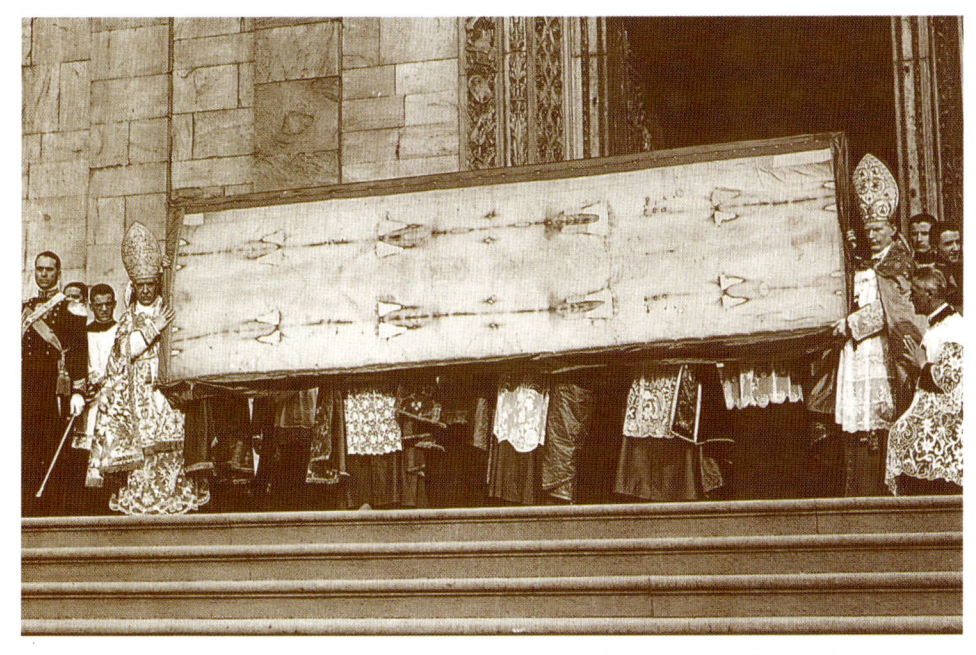

At the end of the Exposition, the Shroud is displayed to the faithful on the Cathedral steps.

Poster of the Exposition.

THE OFFICIAL PHOTOGRAPHS OF 1931

After the sensation caused by the first photographs of 1898, scholars repeatedly asked for further photographs to be taken. The opportunity came with the Exposition of 1931.

The task of photographing the Shroud anew was entrusted to Cav. Giuseppe Enrie.

He produced three photographs of the Shroud full-length, and nine of details. He used nine plates of format 40 x 50 cm, one of 30 x 40 cm, one of 24 x 30 cm and one of 18 x 24 cm.

Cav. Giuseppe Enrie.

The most impressive of the photographs is probably the one of the Holy Face, which Enrie was able to take without the interference of the glass and frame, directly and life-size.

On this page the Holy Face is shown in photographic positive (i.e. as you would see it on the Shroud), and on the opposite page in photographic negative, revealing all the majesty and serenity of the Man of the Shroud.

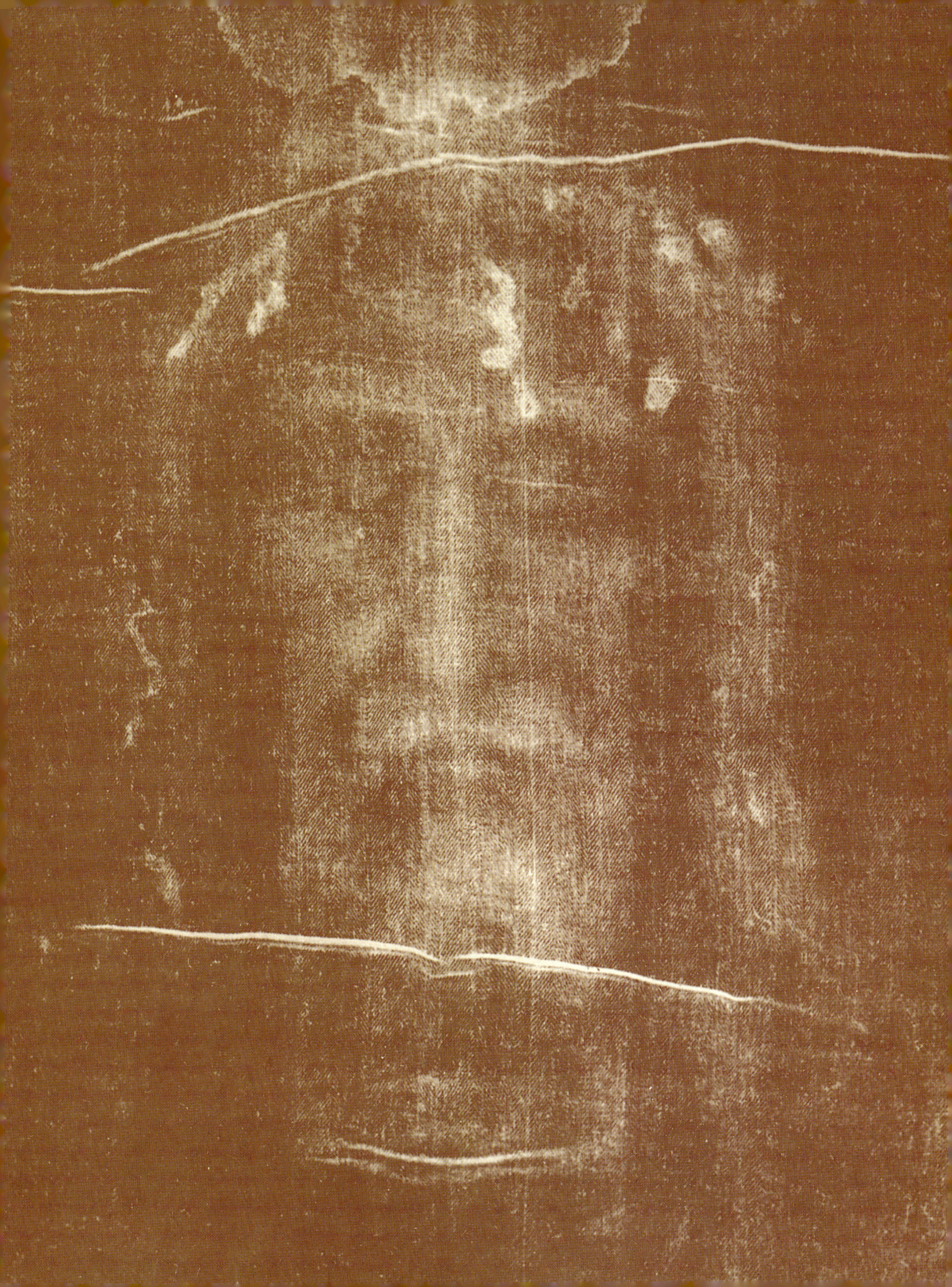

TWO OTHER EXTRAORDINARY PHOTOGRAPHS

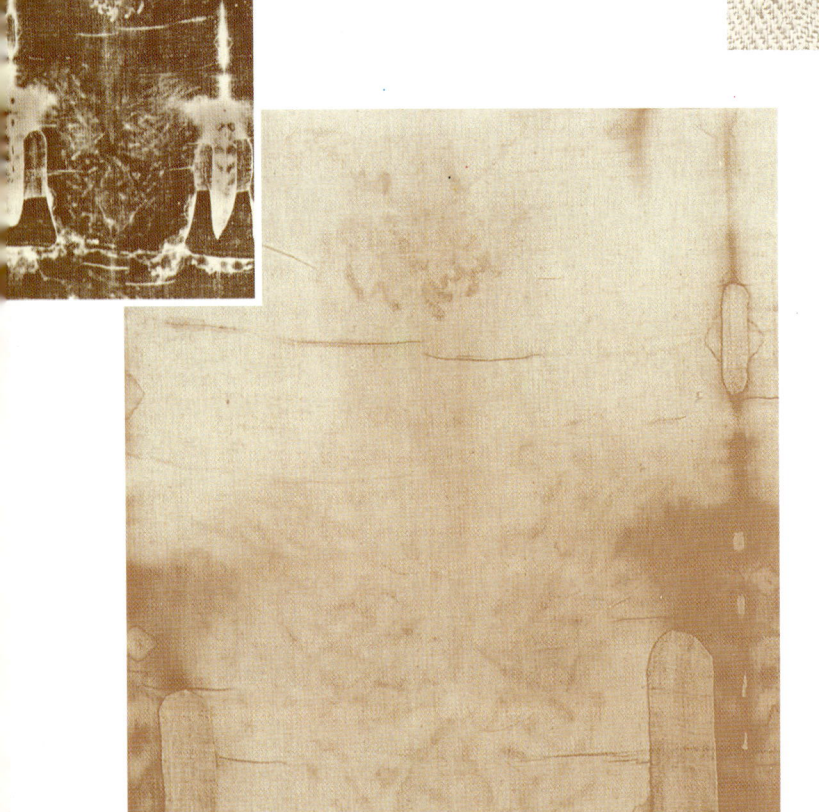

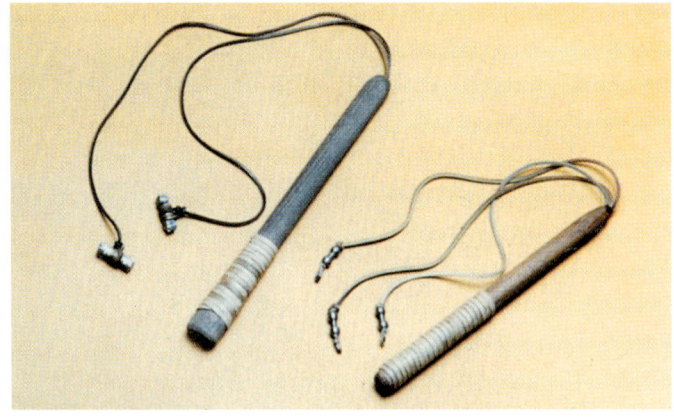

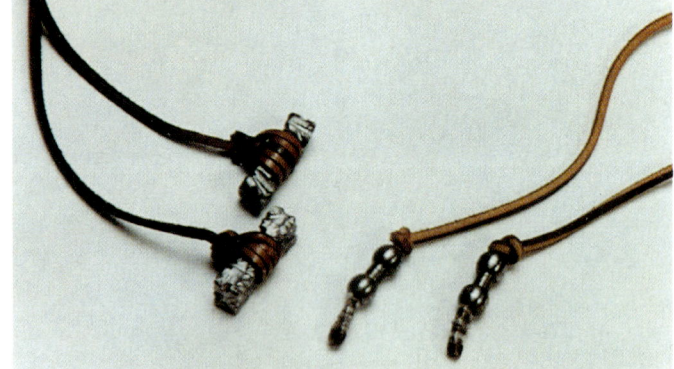

Types of Roman scourge.

THE BACK

This photograph records the awesome number of imprints left by scourge lashes on the Man of the Shroud.
'I must add, only those lashes producing an excoriation or a contusion have left their mark… In all, I have counted more than one hundred of these, perhaps a hundred and twenty' (P. Barbet, *La passione di N. S. Gesù Cristo secondo il chirurgo*, Turin 1951, p. 109).

THE WOUND ON THE LEFT WRIST

This photograph shows the stain caused by blood flowing from the piercing of the left wrist.

Note how subtle the bloody imprint is – impossible for a forger to produce on a cloth as robustly woven as the herringbone material of the Shroud.

To make it easier to study, the photograph has been taken directly, two and a half times linear dimensions, some seven times the actual size of the area.

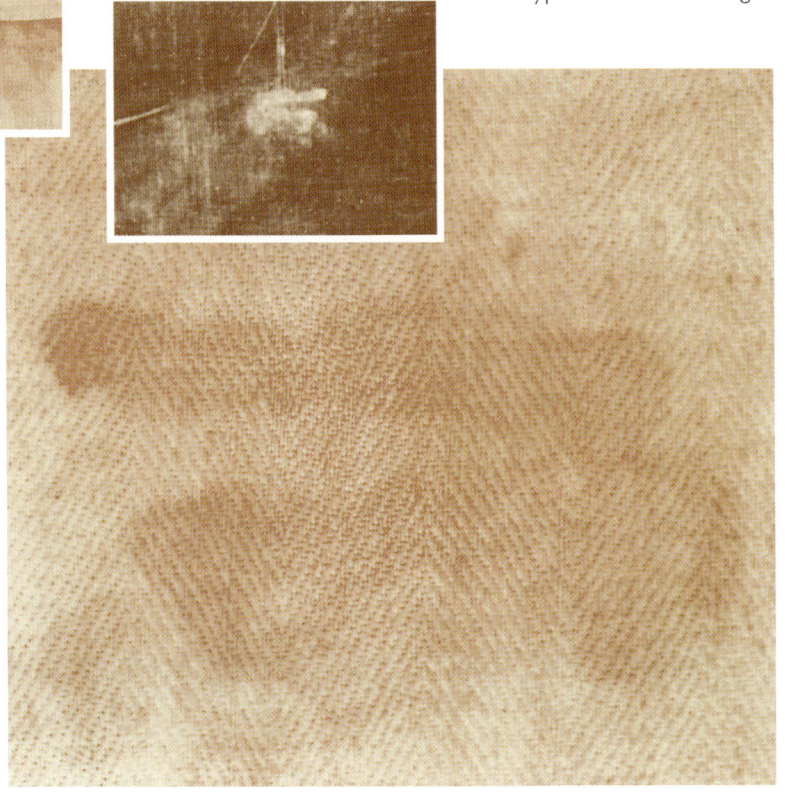

30

The Exposition of 1933

For the special Holy Year proclaimed to mark the 19th centenary of the Redemption to be celebrated as solemnly as possible, another Exposition of the Shroud was held, only three years after the previous one, from September 24 till October 15, by the express wish of Pius XI. It also offered an opportunity to check the accuracy of Enrie's photographs taken of the Shroud in 1931. The extraordinary nature of the Shroud now being generally admitted, there was growing interest in it and a new, stronger impetus given to studies and scientific research on the Sacred Cloth.

Above left: Exposition poster.

Above: The Shroud on the altar of Exposition. Elaborate decorative carving has been added to the frame containing the Shroud.

Bottom left: The frame alone, used in 1931 and 1933, was later placed over the high altar of the church of the Confraternity of the Most Holy Shroud, with a full-size photographic copy of the Holy Shroud in it.

31

1939-1946 – The Shroud at Montevergine

To preserve the Shroud from possible enemy action (war was imminent), it was secretly moved to the Shrine of Montevergine, Avellino. It arrived there on September 25, 1939, after being kept temporarily (18 days) in the chapel of the Royal Palace in Rome.

THE MONASTERY OF THE BENEDICTINES was thought to be the most suitable place for the Shroud on security grounds and also because of the respect due to it. It was feared that not even in the Vatican would it have been safe from enemy action.

Above right: the altar of the Night Choir where the Shroud was kept from September 25, 1939, to October 29, 1946.

Centre: Cardinal Fossati chose to reward the Benedictine monks with a special, very brief Exposition in this hall, for having guarded the Shroud for seven years.

Below: October 31, 1946 – The Shroud is brought back to Turin and reinstalled above Bertola's altar.

> In his pastoral letter of October 31, 1946, Cardinal Maurilio Fossati reminisced: 'It was wise to have taken it away from Turin, since, even if it had been respected by the bombs, it would not perhaps have been respected by the invader, who lost no time in trying to find out where it was.'

The official photographs of 1969
Photos by kind permission of Giovanni Battista Judica Cordiglia

First colour photograph of the Shroud, taken on June 10, 1969, in the 'time-exposure room' set up in the Royal Palace.

During the private inspection held from June 16 to June 18, 1969, the photographer Giovanni Battista Judica Cordiglia was officially entrusted with photographing the Shroud. He took a number of photographs by normal light, Wood's light and infra-red light, in black-and-white, colour and ultra-violet.

G. B. Judica Cordiglia.

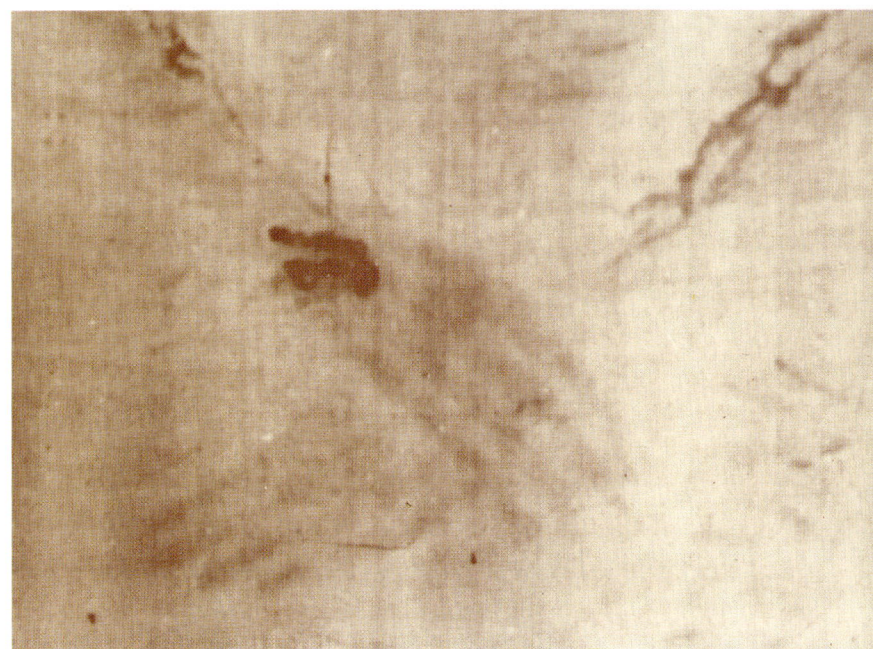

Above centre: macrophotograph of the Shroud fabric.

Above: detail of the hands taken by ultra-violet fluorescence.

Left: the wound in the chest taken from 45 cm away.

1973 – First televised Exposition and first samples taken from the cloth of the Shroud

OCTOBER 4:

- Private Exposition in the Hall of the Swiss in the Royal Palace, Turin, to run tests for the envisaged televised Exposition.

- Checking of the photographs of the Shroud taken by G. B. Judica Cordiglia in 1969.

NOVEMBER 23:

- A further unfolding of the Shroud in the Hall of the Swiss, where it was then shown **for the first time on television**.

- The same evening, with a view to researching accidental pollen grains, Dr Max Frei, founder and director of the Zurich Police Scientific Laboratory, using strips of adhesive tape, took a series of samples of the dust particles deposited on the surface of the Shroud over the years.

NOVEMBER 24:

- For the purpose of **haematological** and **microscopic ultrastructural** research, 9 threads and 6 fragments of thread were taken from the Shroud material, their length varying from 4 to 28 mm.

- For research on the **material** and **structure** of the Shroud, Professor G. Raes (Director of the Ghent Institute of Textile Technology) was assigned two of the aforesaid threads (12 and 13 mm long), plus a sample from the edge of the Sacred Sheet 'triangular in form (a right-angle triangle) with base of 40 mm, the shorter side 13 mm and the hypotenuse 42 mm.'

From: *La S. Sindone – Ricerche e studi della Commissione di Esperti nominate dall'Arcivescovo di Torino. Card. Michele Pellegrino. nel 1969.*

Front and back of the sample of Shroud material examined by Professor G. Raes (*linear dimensions double the original*).

Professor Max Frei at the microscope while examining the photographs of the Shroud on October 4, 1973. On his right, Mgr. Pietro Caramello, Custodian of the Relic, and Professor Aurelio Ghio, his able assistant in scientific research. On Frei's left, Dr Roberto Spigo completes the three-man team of experts for checking the photographs.

1978 – Exposition for 43 days
Direct examination for 120 hours

During the longest Exposition of the Shroud in history – from August 26 to October 8 – more than three million pilgrims, coming from all over the world, were able to venerate the Holy Shroud.

Above left: pilgrims in the Cathedral square waiting to venerate the Shroud.

Above: interior of the Cathedral with the Holy Shroud exposed. In the background, Guarini's chapel and Bertola's altar.

Left: The high altar of Turin Cathedral with the Holy Shroud exposed above it.

THREE STAGES IN LAYING OUT THE SHROUD

For a total of 120 hours from the night of Sunday, October 8, until the evening of the following Friday, October 13, 44 scholars, some Italian, others foreign, conducted direct examinations of the Shroud, which had been stretched out flat on a revolving table suitable for the purpose in the hall of the Royal Palace known as 'the library'.

Altar of the Holy Shroud in the Guarini chapel. Engraving by Lione da Daudet, 1737, printed in Turin by Reycend & Guibert. 29 × 46 cm.

The Shroud is taken down from Bertola's altar by Mgr. Jose Cottino, spread out on the revolving table and fixed at the edges of the cloth.

1980 – The pilgrimage to Turin of Pope John Paul II

The Holy Father himself described it:

'*When at the beginning of September 1978 I went to Turin as a pilgrim anxious to venerate the Holy Shroud – that eminent Relic linked to the mystery of our Redemption – I certainty could not have foreseen, on the morrow of the election of my beloved Predecessor John Paul I that I should come back less than two years later with other responsibilities and in another setting*' (Osservatore Romano, April 14-15, 1980, p.6)

The private Exposition had not been part of the official programme, given the little time available; nonetheless, should the need arise, the necessary preparations had been made, and when it became known that the papal visit had not diverged much from its time-table, steps were immediately taken to open the reliquary and hold the Exposition, of which the two photographs below show two moments.

In the first photograph, Mgr. Caramello points out details on the Shroud to the Holy Father. In the second, the Pope kisses the Shroud.

1983 – From the House of Savoy to the Holy See

In 1452 (or according to some historians 1453) Marguerite de Charny, not wishing to return the Shroud to the Canons of Lirey, who had summoned her before the authorities at Besançon and Troyes to make her give it back to them, ceded the relic to Duke Louis of Savoy and his wife Ann of Cyprus.

The Shroud thus became the property of the House of Savoy for some 530 years, that is to say until the death of King Umberto II (March 18, 1983) when, by that sovereign's will, it passed into the ownership of the Holy See. The deed of gift was signed the following October 18.

Right: meeting between the Holy Father and King Umberto II.

1992 – Inspection of the Shroud to ensure its better conservation

September 7 – Private Exposition and inspection of the Sacred Cloth by experts invited to suggest appropriate measures for guaranteeing its better conservation. Nicola Pisano photographed details of the Shroud which had been chosen by the experts for their individual investigations.

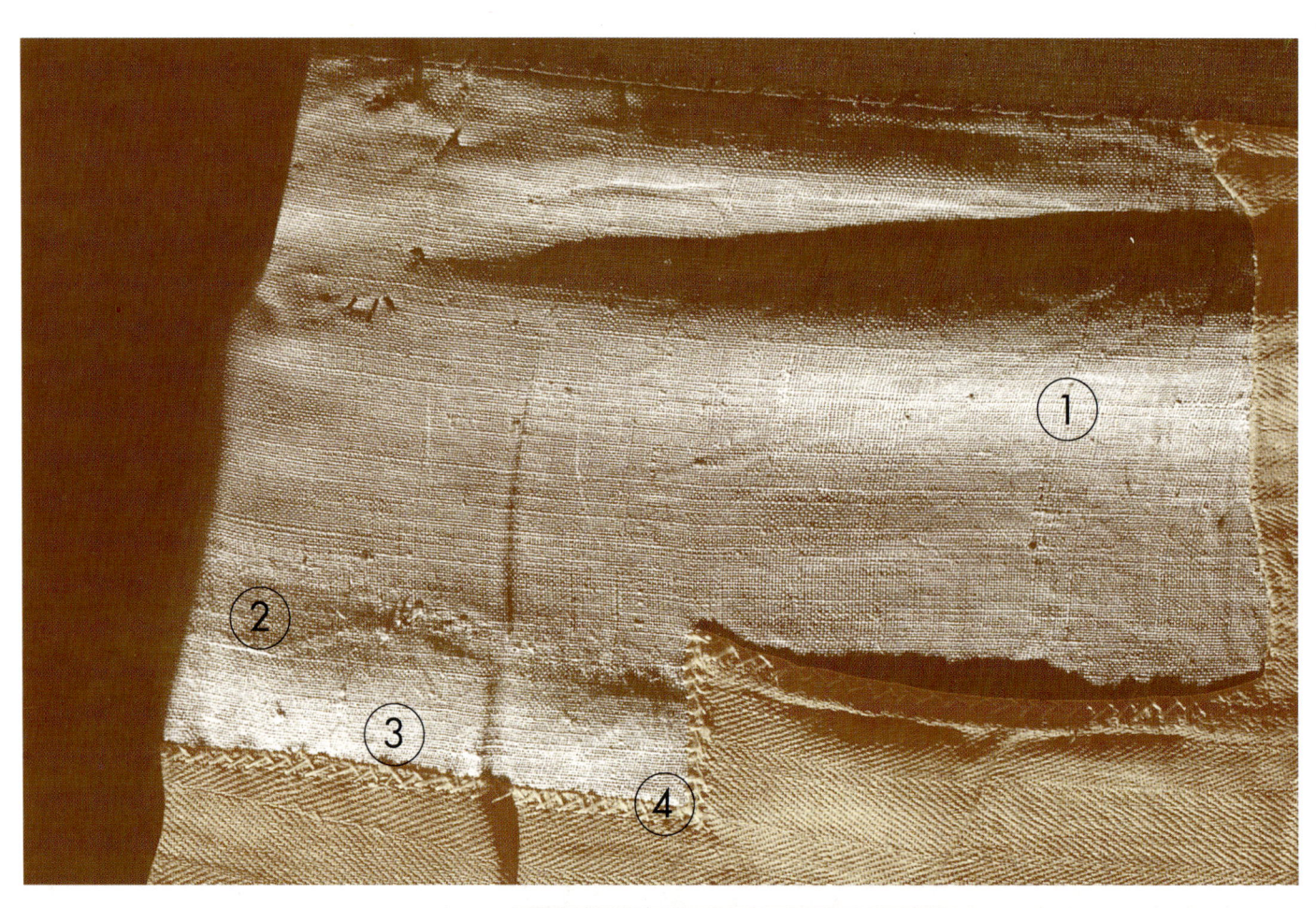

Above: how the upper left edge of the Shroud looks today after removal of the samples for examination. It is easy to single out:
1. the holland backing applied by the Poor Clares of Chambéry in 1534;
2. the darkening of the area where the fragment was removed on which Prof. Raes conducted his material and structural analyses;
3. the sector from which the sample used for radiocarbon dating was taken in 1988;
4. the existing seam between the Sacred Sheet and the holland cloth.

Right: photo of the same sector of the Shroud, taken from Enrie's original photographic plates (1931). When compared with the photograph above, the difference can be seen between its state as it then was, and that subsequent to the removal of the samples.

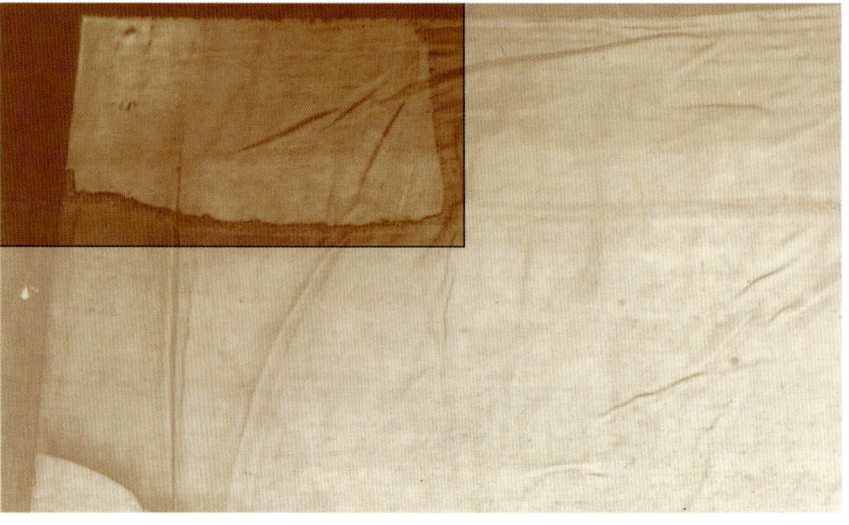

ILLUSTRATIONS OF THE PATCHES SEWN ON THE SHROUD BY THE POOR CLARES OF CHAMBÉRY IN 1534

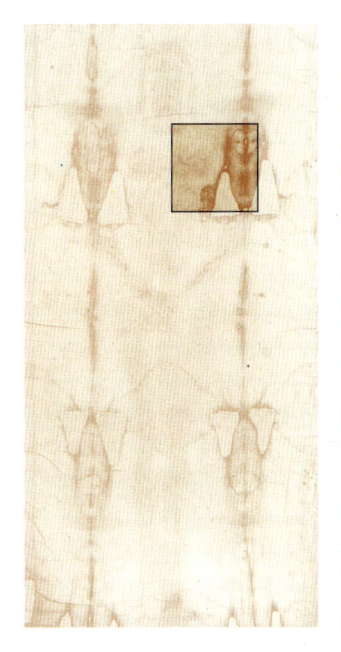

Above: *FRONTAL SECTION* – Upper part of the patch partially covering the bloodstain corresponding to the wound in the chest. The patch has been re-sewn, probably by the Blessed Valfrè, at the points where it had come away from the underlying holland cloth.

Below: *DORSAL SECTION* – Two patches applied at the level of the calves of the Man of the Shroud.

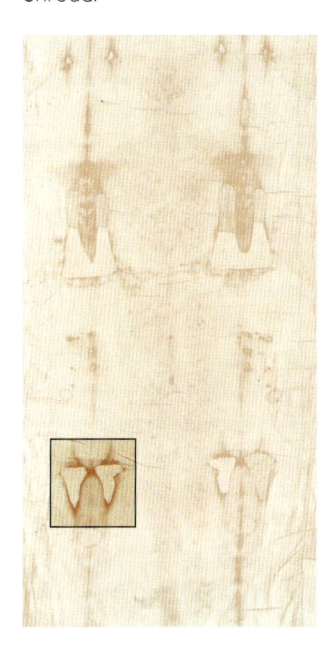

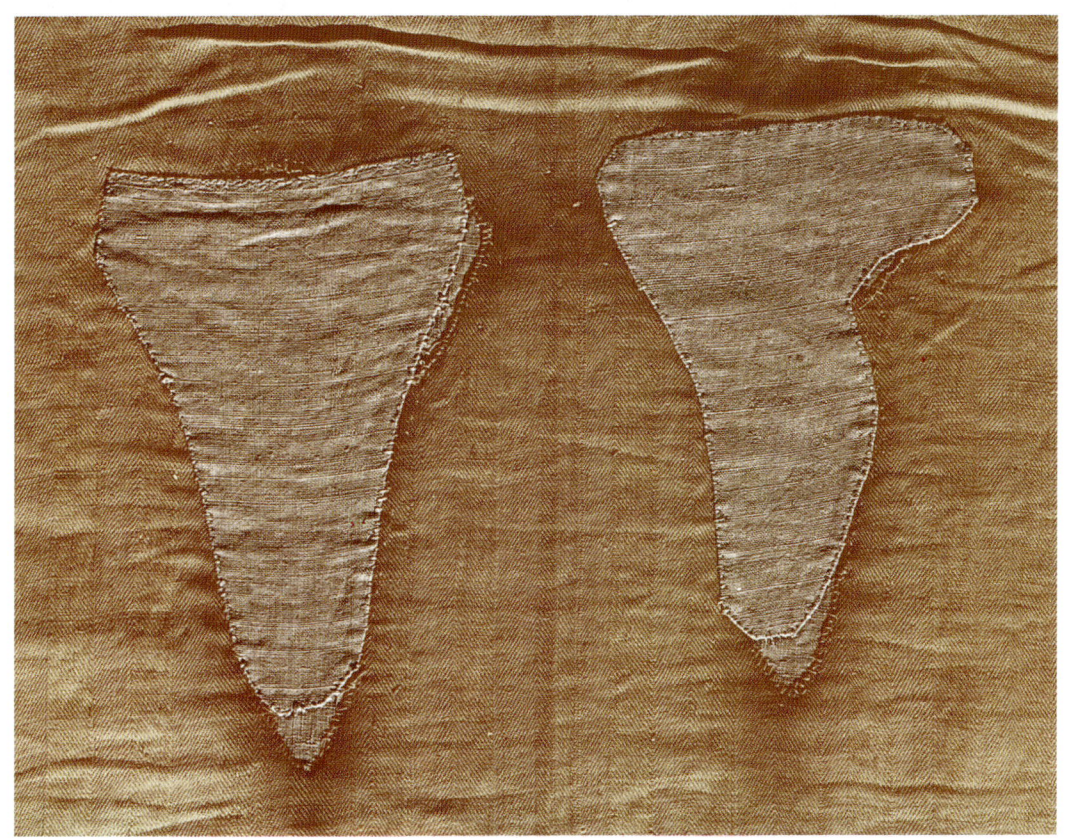

1993 – The Shroud is temporarily moved

On February 24, 1993, when restoration work on the Guarini Chapel could no longer be postponed – its structure was in such a poor state of repair as to be positively dangerous – the Holy Shroud was temporarily moved to the adjacent nave of Turin Cathedral and put immediately behind the high altar in the centre of the Canons' choir.

A vertical transparent case, designed by the architect Andrea Bruno, was constructed from thick plates of bullet-proof glass, guaranteeing resistance to traumatic shock or malicious attack. The extreme simplicity of the case is intended to concentrate the visitor's attention on the box containing the relic and encourage recollectedness in the faithful.

Saved from the flames for the third time
On the night of April 11-12, 1997, a fearsome fire devastated the Chapel of the Shroud and the adjoining tower of the Royal Palace, threatening the Canons' choir in Turin Cathedral where the Shroud was being kept.

With great difficulty, a team of the Turin Fire Service (the 21st) managed to break open the bullet-proof glass case and carry the Shroud to safety.

Two days after this disastrous event, the Commission for the conservation of the Shroud was able to announce that no damage had been caused to the sacred sheet.

The bullet-proof case as it stood in the Canon's choir (Photo P. Mussa).

SCIENTIFIC RESEARCH

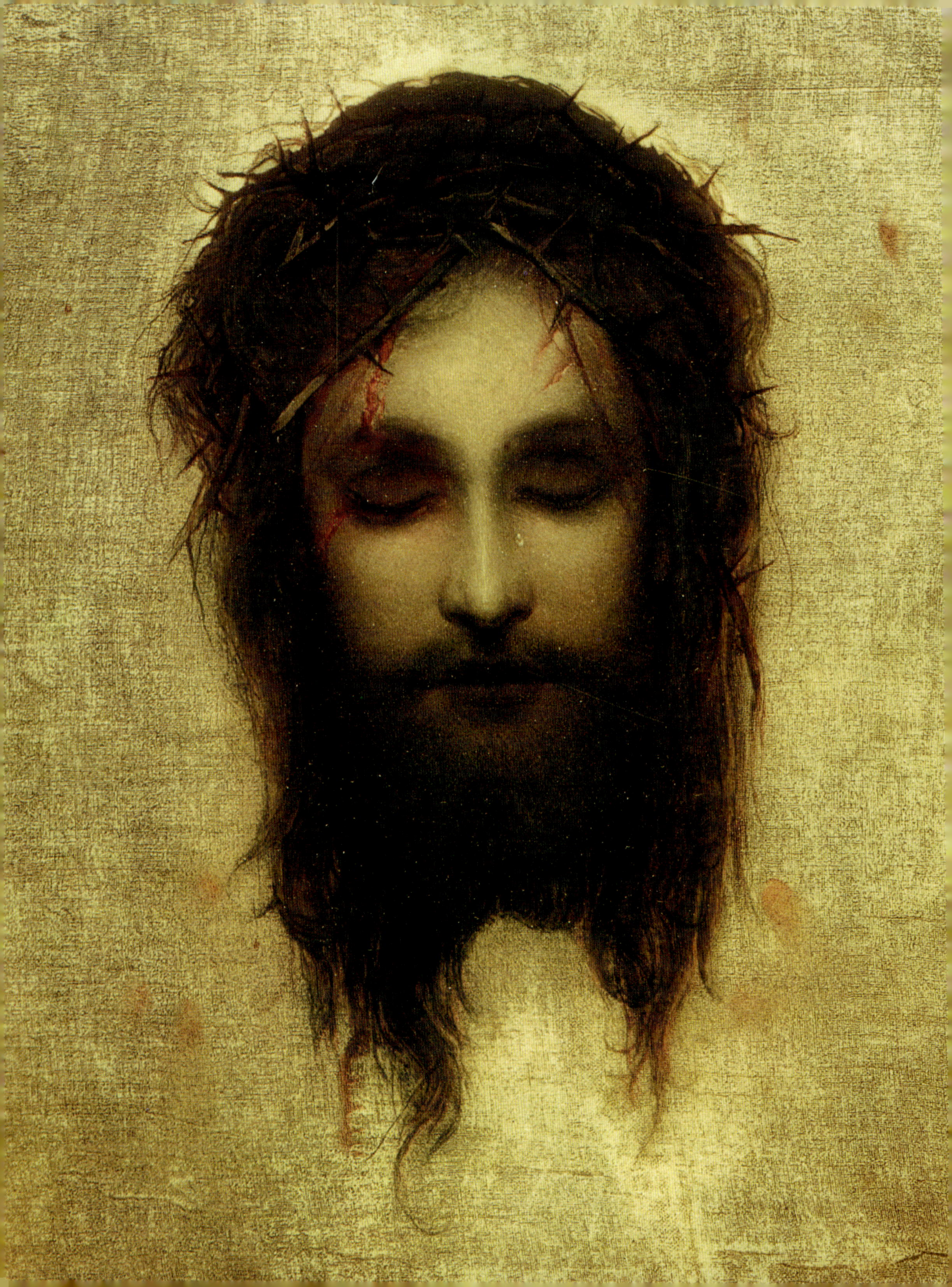

1969 – For the first time the Shroud examined by scientific experts

Private Exposition, June 16-18, 1969, in the Chapel of the Crucifix in the Royal Palace, Turin, for the Sacred Cloth to be inspected by the Commission of Experts nominated by Cardinal Michele Pellegrino.

Purposes of the examination:
– to assess its state of preservation;
– to make suggestions for its future conservation;
– to advise on possible examinations and future lines of research.

During the investigation the Experts had time to make a direct study of the Shroud by naked eye and also under the microscope.

Proposal and requests from the Experts

Having reported on its excellent state of preservation, the Experts recommended that future research should be directed along the following lines:
- ascertainment of the (at least) probable date of the cloth and the patches by archaeological inquiry and, if necessary, by physical and chemical means;
- ascertainment of the various components present in the different coloured imprints on the linen;
- survey of the Shroud's weight section by section;
- examination of the entire sheet by a range of optical methods (photography, microphotography, spectroscopic analysis);
- textile analysis.

At the end of their inspection they recommended for immediate action:
- taking off the white cloth backing through which the patches had been sewn, but leaving the patches themselves intact;
- taking minute samples (for micro-identification) for physical and chemical analysis, textile analysis & c.

(From: *La S. Sindone - Ricerche e studi della Commissione di Esperti nominate dall'Arcivescovo di Torino. Card. Michele Pellegrino*, in 1969).

On opposites page: Face by unknown artist.

Above: Cardinal M. Pellegrino's press conference.

Centre: the Commission of Experts round the Shroud.

Below: the table and frame used for stretching out the Cloth. (Photos by kind permission of G. B. Judica Cordiglia).

Studies on the origin of the imprints

Having discovered that the Shroud imprints were *negative* images and having ruled out any likelihood of their being so due to some phenomenon's having caused the colour inversion of an originally *positive* image, Professor Paul Vignon in 1901 formulated the so-called 'vaporographic' theory.

According to this, the negative images of the body of the Man of the Shroud had been imprinted on the Sheet by the reaction of the aloes (mixed with myrrh) with which the corpse had been smeared, and its resulting transformation into a colourant due to the abundant emanation of ammoniacal fumes produced by fermentation of the urea contained in the blood and sweat.

This theory was revived, with modifications, by new experiments conducted by Professors Ruggero Romanese (1939) and Giovanni Judaica Cordiglia (1941), by Don Gaetano Intriglio, Mario Moroni and in particular by Dr Sebastiano Rodante.

Right: experimental tests by:

1. – R. Romanese
2 – G. Judica Cordiglia
3 – G. Intrigillo
4 – M. Moroni
5 & 6 – S. Rodante

Origin of the image

For Dr Ray Rogers of the Los Alamos National Scientific Laboratory '... the most likely hypothesis is that the images are due to a discoloration of thermal origin, or to some kind of burn.' This thesis has been proved to be without foundation by later research (Moroni, Rodante, Intriglio).

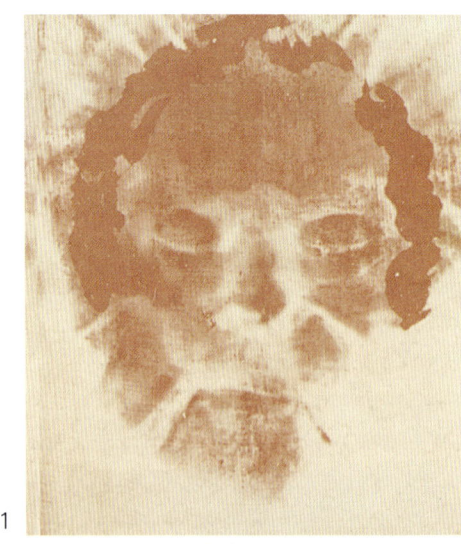

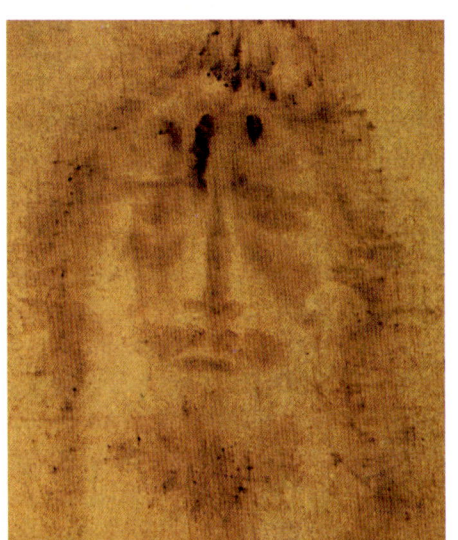

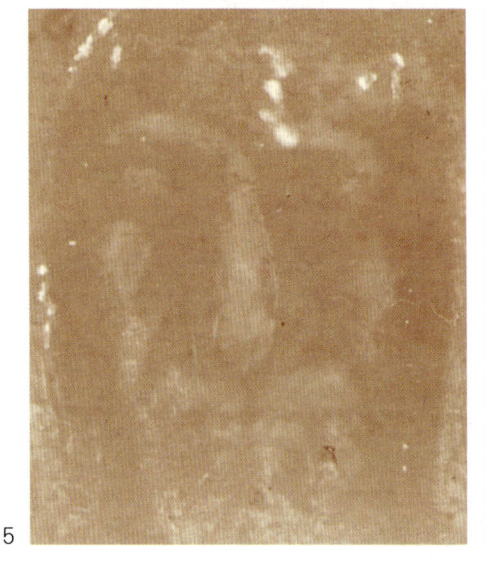

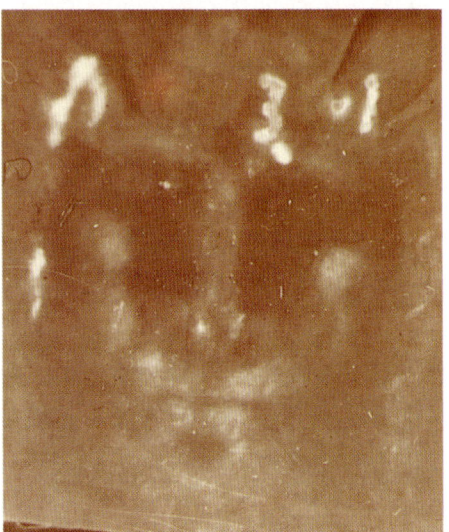

Study of the image

The research scholars Don Lynn and Jean Lorre of Pasadena's Jet Propulsion Laboratory (NASA), California, have demonstrated 'that the image has no preferred directionality. This proves that the Shroud image cannot be the work of an artist, for he would have used the conventional technique of brush-strokes.'

Density characteristics of the image

Drs John P. Jackson and Eric J. Jumper of the Airforce Academy, Colorado, state 'that there is a mathematical correlation between image intensity and cloth to body distance which is characteristic of the Shroud image' and gives us the remarkable result of a three-dimensional image of the Man of the Shroud. This characteristic three-dimensional image is either absent or distorted in normal photographic images or in paintings, hence no artist of the fourteenth century could have introduced information of this sort into his work, not having had any possibility of encountering it.

After 1978 the research team of STURP (Shroud of Turin Research Project) concluded that the image had been caused by a localised modification of the cellulose component in the flax. What caused this change? Baima Bollone wonders if it may not have been the very preservatives (aloes and myrrh) of which traces have been found on the Shroud linen.

1976 – Reports of the Experts

Haematological research – In their final report, the team of Giorgio Frache, Eugenia Mari-Rizzati and Emilio MARI maintain:
'… generic tests of species by grouping (these last limited to the ABO system) have yielded a negative result.'
However, '… the negative response to the tests carried out does *not* permit an *absolute* judgement ruling out the haematic nature of the matter examined.'

Microscopic and ultra-structural research – Professors Guido Filogama and Alberto Zina end their report by stating:
'Observation by optical microscope has not revealed corpuscles identifiable as red blood-cells,' but that 'there may be red cells cannot be excluded with absolute certainty,' whereas '… new and possibly more significant data might be furnished by study of the threads by scanning microscope.'

Research on textile structure – Professor G. RAES in concluding his report states that, on the basis of observations made, he can say there is no precise indication that would allow him to affirm with certainty whether the Shroud textile *may* or *may not* be datable to the time of Christ.

From: *La S. Sindone – Ricerche e studi della Commissione di Esperti nominate dall'Arcivescovo di Torino, Card. Michaele Pellegrino, in 1969.*

Pollen research – Studies made of the dust adhering to the surface of the Shroud permitted Dr Max Frei to draw the following initial conclusions:

…. presence on the Sheet of pollen grains from desert plants that grow in Palestine.

The pollen most common on the Sheet is identical with the pollen most common in the sediments of Lake Gennesaret in those sedimentary strata which are 2,000 years old.

Another specimen comes from Asia Minor and more precisely from the neighbourhood of Constantinople, while a great number of grains have originated in France and Italy.

It is therefore logical to deduce, in the light of the evidence acquired, that the historical and geographical life of the Shroud reflects the migrations which it has undergone over the centuries.

From: *Sindon*, booklet no. 23 of April 1976.

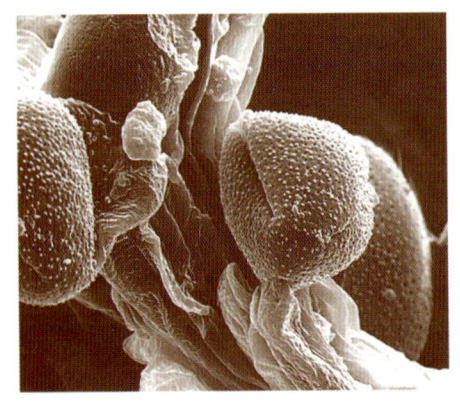

Pterantus Dichotomus Forsk.

Phillyrea Angustifolia.

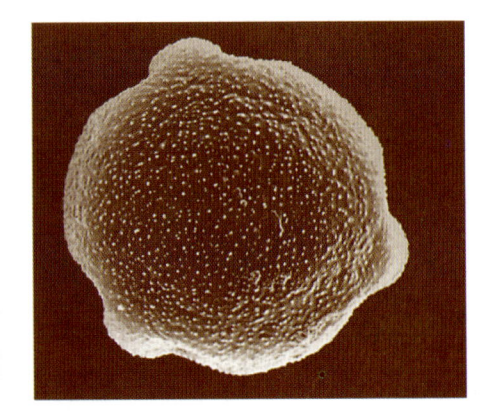

Corylus Avellana L.

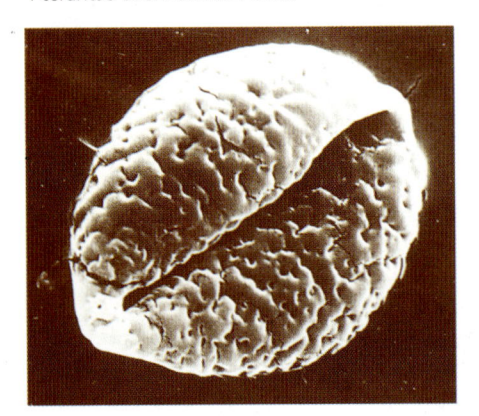

Prosopic Facta Macbr.

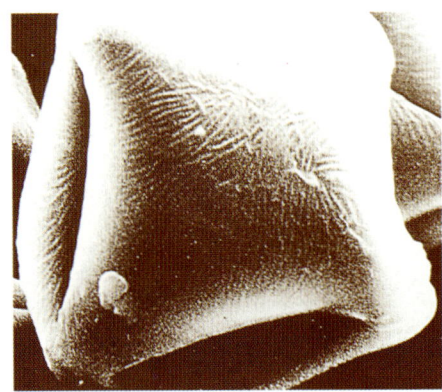

Haplophillum Tuberculatum Juss.

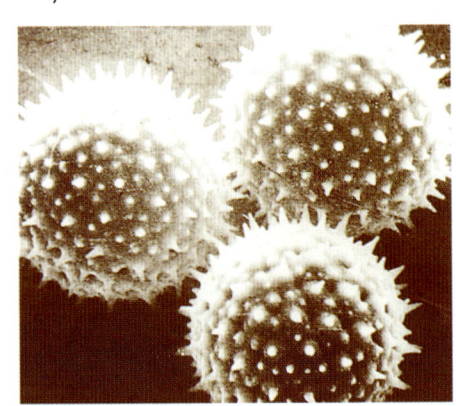

Althea Officinalis Marsh.

Study and research

1978

To complete his investigations begun in 1973 into the pollens present on the Shroud, Dr Max Frei took some twenty more pollen samples.

For haematological research, Prof. Pierluigi Baima Bollone extracted 12 samples of thread from warp and weft, not longer than 2 cm, from different predetermined points (clean linen, stains thought to be blood, image); he also removed 4 threads sticking out of the Cloth with one end free. The threads were removed, among other reasons, so that they could be 'submitted to analysis by electron microscope and neutronic activation.'

To be able to photograph the hidden side of the Shroud (covered by the holland cloth backing to which the Poor Clares of Chambéry had sewn the Shroud in 1534 to strengthen it) and to take samples of the dusts deposited there over the centuries, four seams were unpicked along the edges of the Shroud. Professors Maria Artom and Paolo Soardo made a survey of the colour co-ordinates so as to monitor any photometric and colorimetric changes possibly occurring in the future.

The American scholars associated in STURP (The Shroud of Turin Research Project, inc.) undertook various types of research, among which were:

- detailed photographic and microphotographic studies;
- complete radiography of the Shroud;
- inspections by infra-red rays;
- study of the spectrum of light given off by fluorescence;
- collecting dust samples for biological and chemical analysis;
- survey of the spectrum of X-rays given off from various characteristic points.

(From: *Sindon* 28/1979, pp. 13-14).

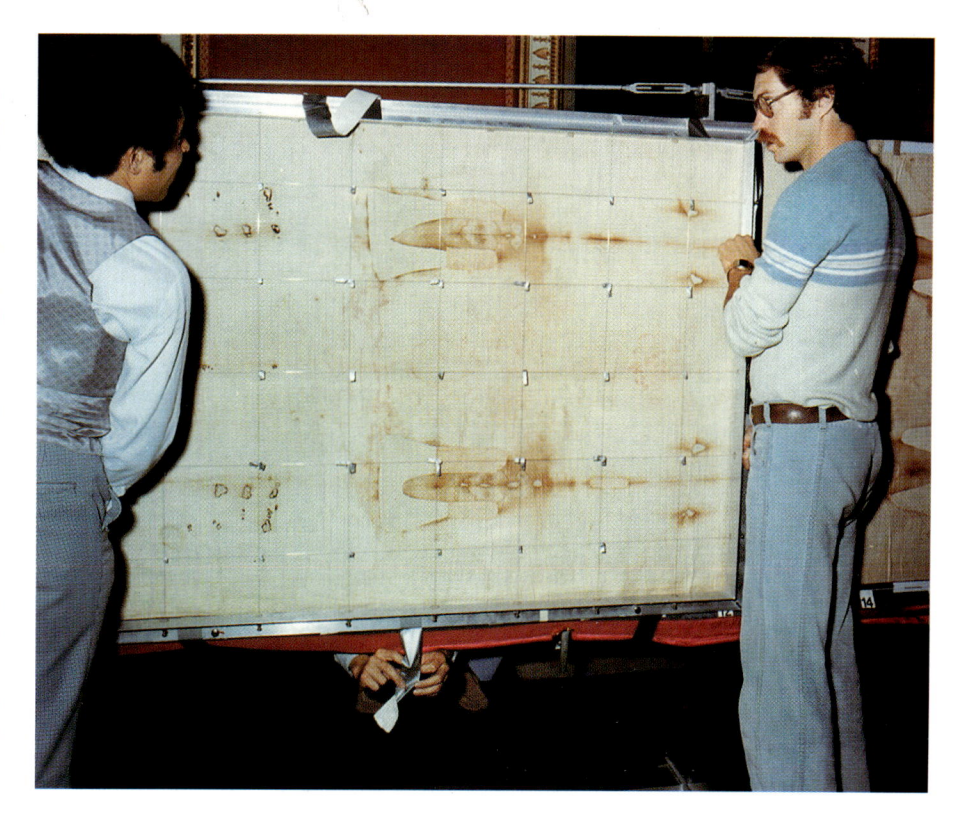

TRACES OF BLOOD ON THE SHROUD

The Sacred Sheet displays the body of a man with many traumatic injuries and with stains that tradition has always held to be blood, in substantial agreement with the Gospel story.

In recent years, medical science has confirmed this:

May 1950

At the First International Convention of Studies on the Holy Shroud, the French surgeon, Dr Pierre Barbet of the Hôpital S. Joseph, Paris, presented a report dealing with the characteristic appearance of the finest details of the stains supposed to be of blood, and having as its subject *Proof of the Shroud's authenticity in its bloodstains* (cf *Sindon* 14-15/1970, pp. 21-43).

August 1980

The U.S. research scientists J. H. Heller and A. D. Adler reported that they had succeeded in obtaining significant conversion phenomena of the porphyrin on an adhesive strip applied to the surface of the Sacred Sheet in 1978, corresponding to a spot stained presumably with the blood of the Man of the Shroud (cf Baima Bollone, *Sindone o no*, S.E.I., Turin 1990, p. 190).

This is confirmation of Barbet's views and also rectification (though regarded as a possibility by the original authors) of the negative results of the tests performed in 1976 by FRACHE, MARI-RIZATI and MARI.

The 6 photos of the 1978 Exposition by the architect M. Momo (pp 35/36) are reproduced by kind permission of the Archbishop of Turin.

May 1981

Professor Pierluigi Baima Bollone, surgeon and Professor of Forensic Medicine at the University of Turin, addressing the Medical Academy of Turin, stated that 'his own forensic research on threads taken from the Shroud (in 1978) has led to the identification of traces of aloes, myrrh and blood (Journal of the Medical Academy of Turin – Anno CXLIV – 1981).

August 1981

The American Dr A. D. Adler at a meeting of the Canadian Society of Forensic Sciences reported results analogous to those of Baima Bollone, obtained by analysing adhesive strips applied to the surface of the Shroud in 1978 (cf Baima Bollone, *L'impronta di Dio*, Mondadori Milan 1985, p. 141).

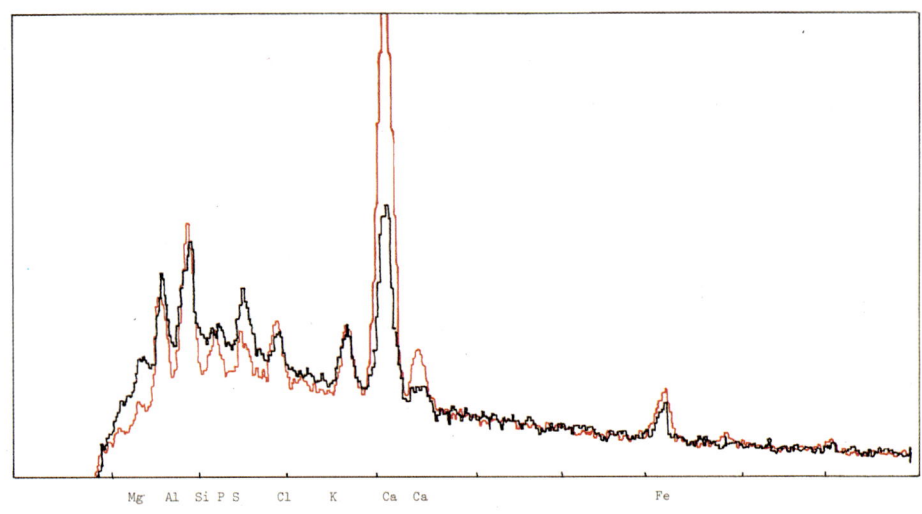

Comparison of microspectrophotometric profile of C 9 d (in red) and that obtained with an experimental stain of blood, aloes, myrrh and saponin on cloth. The inorganic composition is identical.

December 1981

Baima Bollone, Jorio and Massaro, using the fluorescent antibodies method, demonstrate that the haematic traces on threads taken in 1978 are those of human blood. See *Sindon* 30/1981, pp. 5-8, from which we reprint the following study by Baima Bollone:

MAP OF THE SHROUD DIVIDED INTO 48 SUB-SECTIONS

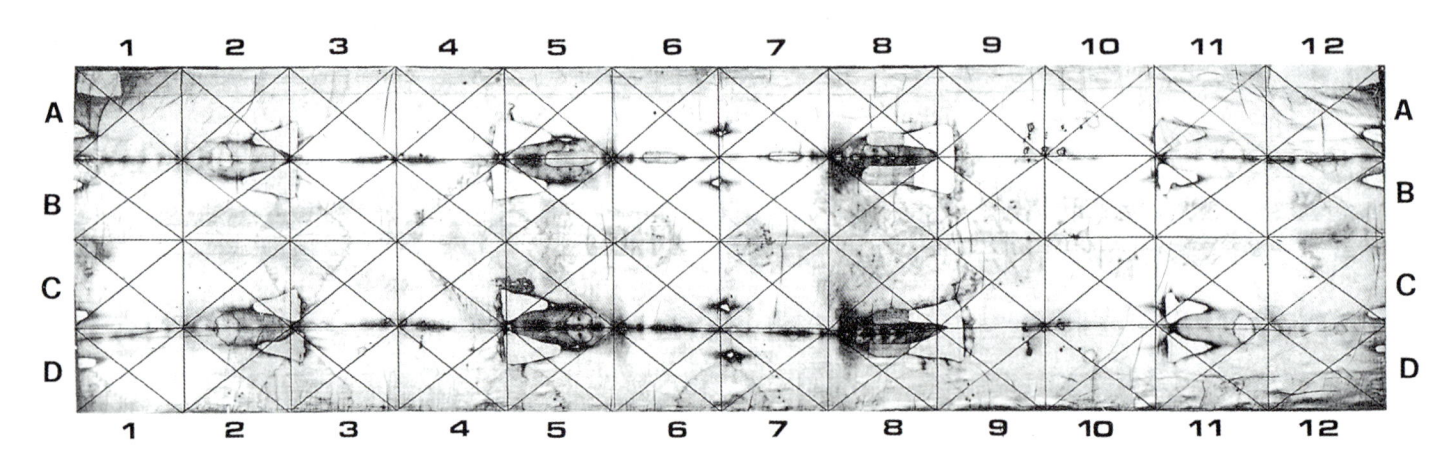

To make details easier to identify, the 48 sub-divisions of the above 'map' have themselves been sub-divided into sectors a, b, c, d.

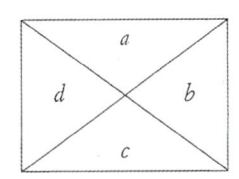

CAPTIONS TO THE PLATES ON PAGE 49

1. view of threads extracted from B 12 c: 10 x original size

2. enlargement 40 x original of one of the said threads by infrared light; in this enlargement already details can be seen of matter superimposed on the linen fibres of the threads.

3. charred fibre from the outer edge: microphotography in polarised light 800 x original.

4. granules of matter constituting the stains in B 12 c; microphotography by transmitted-light photography 800 x original.

5. experimental stain: view of myrrh under the phase-contrast microscope 600 x original.

6. microphotography under phase-contrast microscope of fibres from B 12 c; note the blobs of matter morphologically identical to myrrh; 600 x original.

7. fluorescent microscopy of fibres taken from B 12 e, after incubation with anti human gamma-globular serum with fluorescent tag; 600 x original.

8. ditto, by indirect method (cf text); 800 x original.

49

December 1982

The same Italian research team (Baima Bollone, Jorio and Massaro) using the investigative method of 'mixed agglutination' reached the conclusion that 'the traces of blood on the Shroud now examined by us belong to Group A B' (*Sindon* 31/1982, pp. 5-9).

Identification of the group to which the traces of blood on the Shroud belong

Plate 1 – Mixed agglutination. Negative field on 'white' Shroud fibres incubated with anti-A and cemented with erythrocytes A; 600 x original.

Plate 2 – Mixed agglutination. Negative field on 'white' Shroud fibres: incubated with anti-B and cemented with erythrocytes B; 600 x original.

Plate 3 – Mixed agglutination. Large agglutinations of erythrocytes Al, after incubation with anti-A; 800 x original.

Plate 4 – Mixed agglutination. Large agglutinations of erythrocytes B after incubation with anti-B; 800 x original.

Plate 5 – Mixed agglutination. Agglutination to the surface of fibres on the periphery of the compound (anti-A / erythrocites Al); 800 x original.

Plate 6 – Mixed agglutination. Agglutination to the surface of fibres on the periphery of the compound (anti-B / erythrocytes B); 800 x original.

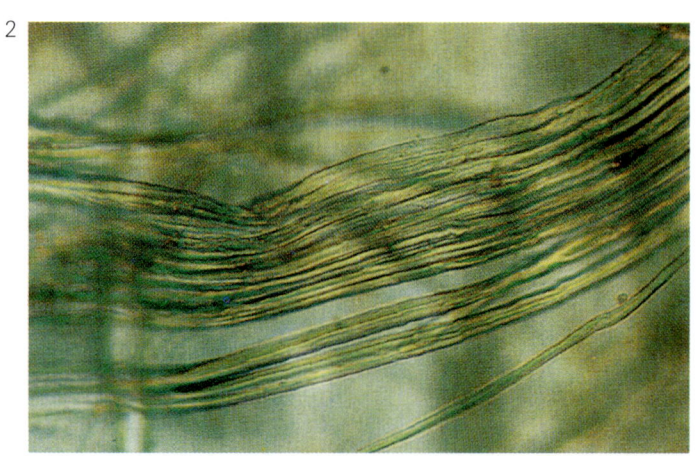

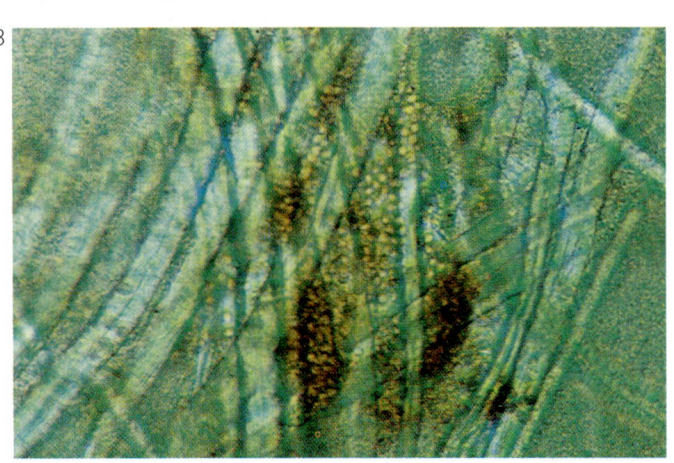

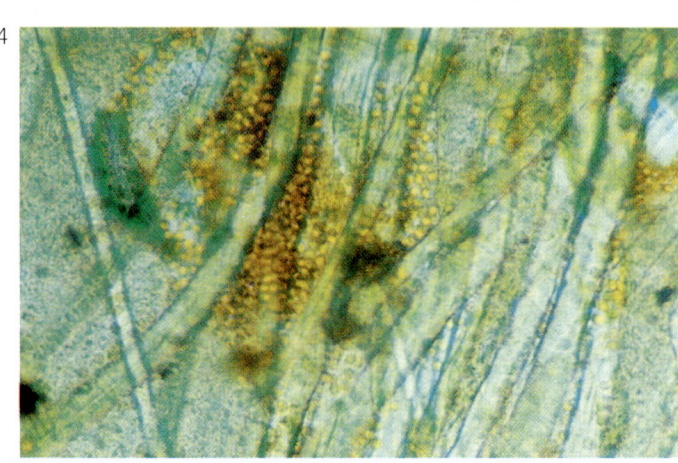

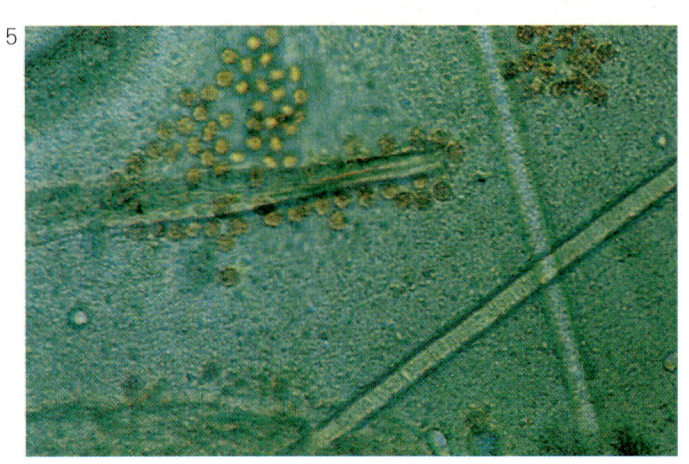

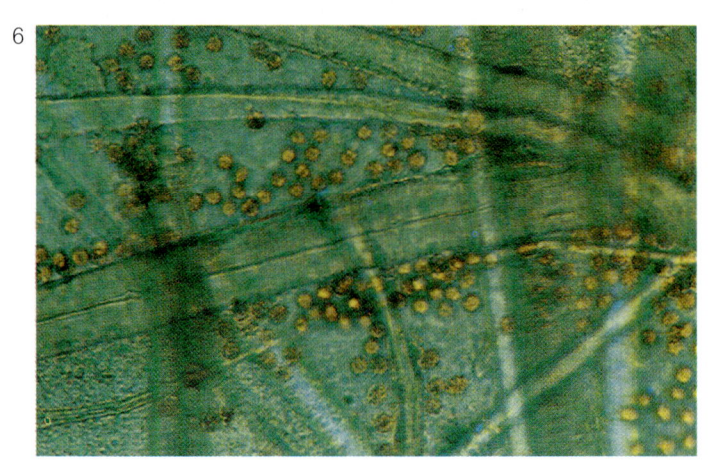

The Shroud and information technology

Information technology has made a remarkable contribution to sindonological studies by providing definitive tests for explaining the nature of the images on the sacred Cloth. By digitising the Shroud image for computer enhancement, it has been possible, by special mathematical procedures, to extract three-dimensional information, thus proving that the imprint on the Sheet was produced by a human body. By computer it has also been possible to show details invisible to the naked eye, thus demonstrating that the Shroud cannot be a painting, given the impossibility of representing pictorially what the eye itself cannot see.

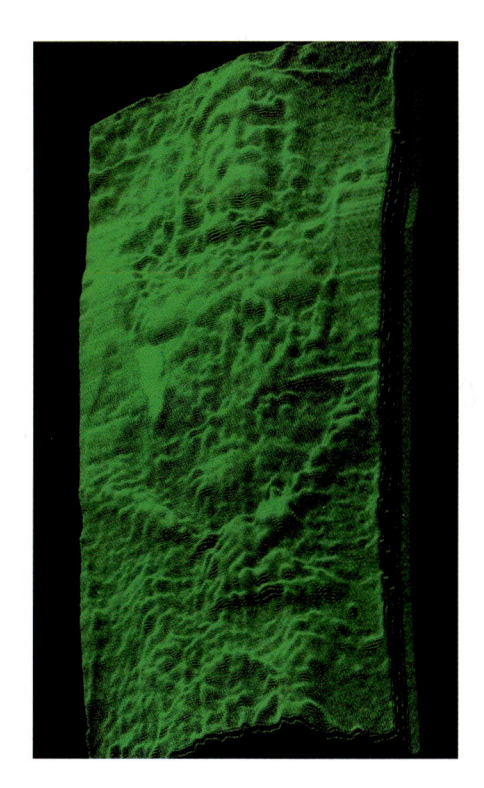

The U.S. scientists Jumper and Jackson were the first to obtain a three-dimensional image of the body and face of the Man of the Shroud. Later, Prof Giovanni Tamburelli (1923-1990) of the University of Turin – with the help of a CSELT team of the IRI-STET group – was to obtain a sharper three-dimensional image, with a wealth of important detail.

Next, by three-dimensional enhancement, Prof Tamburelli and Prof N. Balossino of the Department of Information Technology, University of Turin, produced the wonderful pictures reproduced here.

Left: three-dimensional image of the front of the Man of the Shroud's tortured body.
Above: his face.
Below: the same image of the face after removal of the wounds by information techniques.

Small coins on the eyes

In 1979, Prof Fr Francis L. Filas, SJ discovered the outline of a small coin on the right eyelid of the Man of the Shroud a *lituus*. Subsequently, the sindonologist and numismatical expert Mario Moroni has proposed it should be identified as a *dilepton lituus*, struck by Pontius Pilate at the end of AD 29.

Dilepton lituus.

In 1996 Profs P. L. Baima Bollone and N. Balossino announced that on the arch of the left eyebrow they had detected the outline of a coin later identified as a *lepton simpulum*, also struck by Pilate in AD 29.

Lepton simpulum.

Is the Shroud the iconographical model for ancient pictures of Jesus?

History is largely based on documents, and these can be either written or representational, recording or depicting someone or something in the past. Iconography thus is an historical document too.

Take for instance the *umbella* (liturgical umbrella) used by Pope John VII (705-707), reproduced in a drawing by the archivist Grimaldi early in the seventeenth century. There the Saviour is shown inside his burial *loculus*, laid out as he appears on the Shroud.

This fact, even if it does not constitute absolutely conclusive proof that the Sacred Sheet is genuine, leads us nonetheless to think that this representation on the *umbella* must in some way have been related to the mysterious figure on the Shroud; which also leads us to suppose that some relic of this sort could have been seen by the *umbella's* designer (Ceccarelli C., *La S. Sindone nelle ricerche moderne*, L.I.C.E., 143-165

Drawing of the *umbella* of Pope John VII made by the archivist Jacopo Grimaldi early in the 17th century, with (below) an unusual representation of the dead Christ, earlier than the late-Byzantine treatments of the same subject. (Rome, St Peter's in the Vatican).

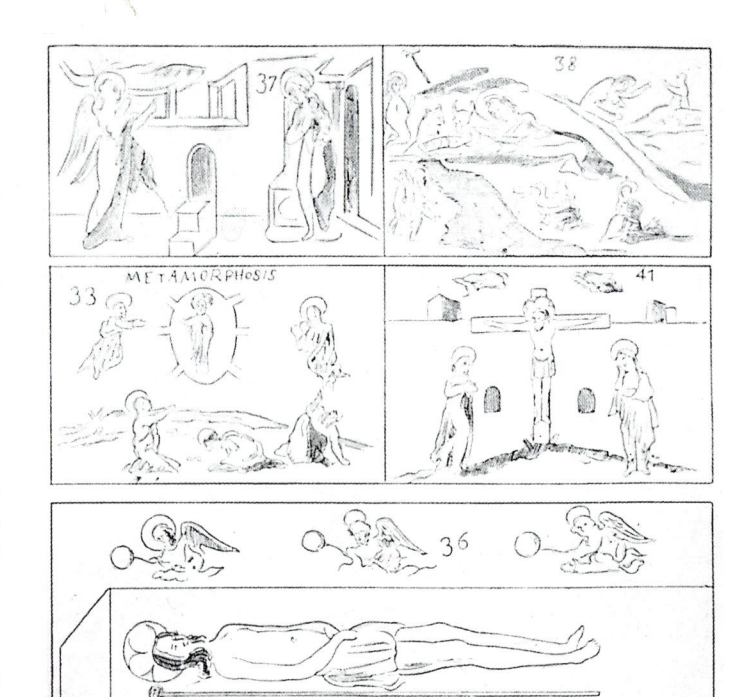

According to the sindonologist Mario Moroni, a numismatics specialist, the Shroud was widely known before the year 1000 AD. He demonstrates the resemblance between the images shown on Byzantine gold coins and the Shroud face which was almost certainly their archetype.

Byzantine coin of 692 AD and the Holy Face on the Shroud. Comparison shows they have the following features in common:

1. Lock of hair in centre of forehead, possibly representing the trickle of blood seen on the Shroud face.

2. Unusual rendering of Christ's face, the ears concealed by hair, as on the Shroud.

Byzantine coin of 869 AD

Image of Christ enthroned; he has a thin foot turned outwards at an angle of 90° from the other. Representation of this abnormality may be due to misinterpretation of the lower limbs of the Man of the Shroud, who appears to have one leg shorter than the other.

Recent computerised studies by Prof. Nello Balossino of the Department of Information Technology, Turin University, seem to show that several faces of Christ produced in the first millennium of the Christian era may have been derived from the Shroud image.

In the four examples reproduced below, where the features of these ancient depictions have been superimposed on the Shroud face, the matching may suggest as much.

1988 – Examination of samples from the Shroud by Radio Carbon

On April 12, 1988, a sample of cloth was taken from the upper left edge of the Shroud. On November 24, 1973, a fragment had already been taken from the same area and submitted to Prof. G. Raes for textile-structural analysis.
The 1988 sample measured 8.1 x 1.6 cm (report of Prof. Dr Franco Testore to the 'Paris International Scientific Symposium on the Shroud of Turin', of September 1989), reduced to 7 x 1 cm after removal of the frayed bits round the edges.

This was then divided into two roughly equal parts, one of which was retained, and the other subdivided into three. Each of the three laboratories (selected from the seven under consideration) i.e. of the University of Oxford (Great Britain), of the University of Arizona (USA) and of the

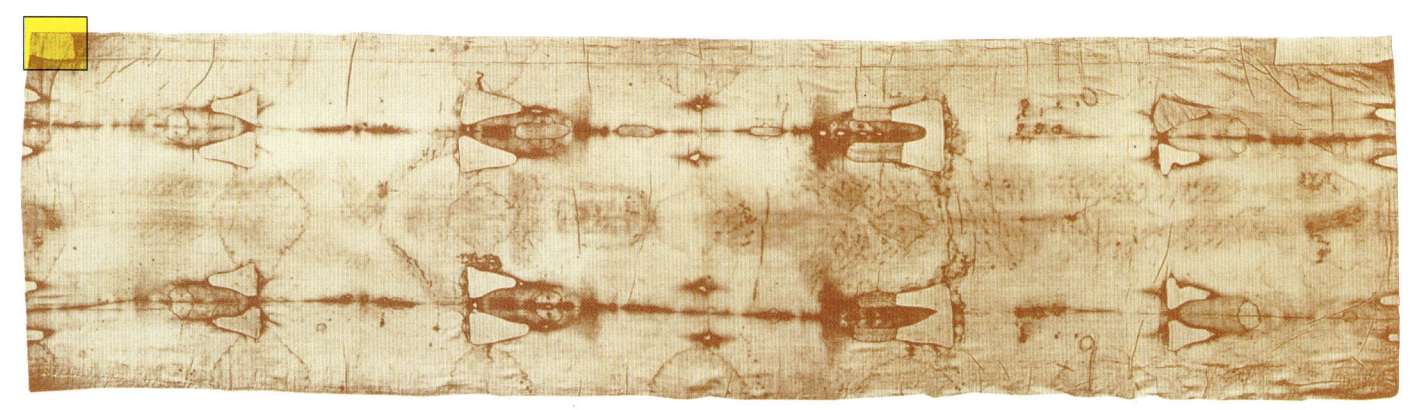

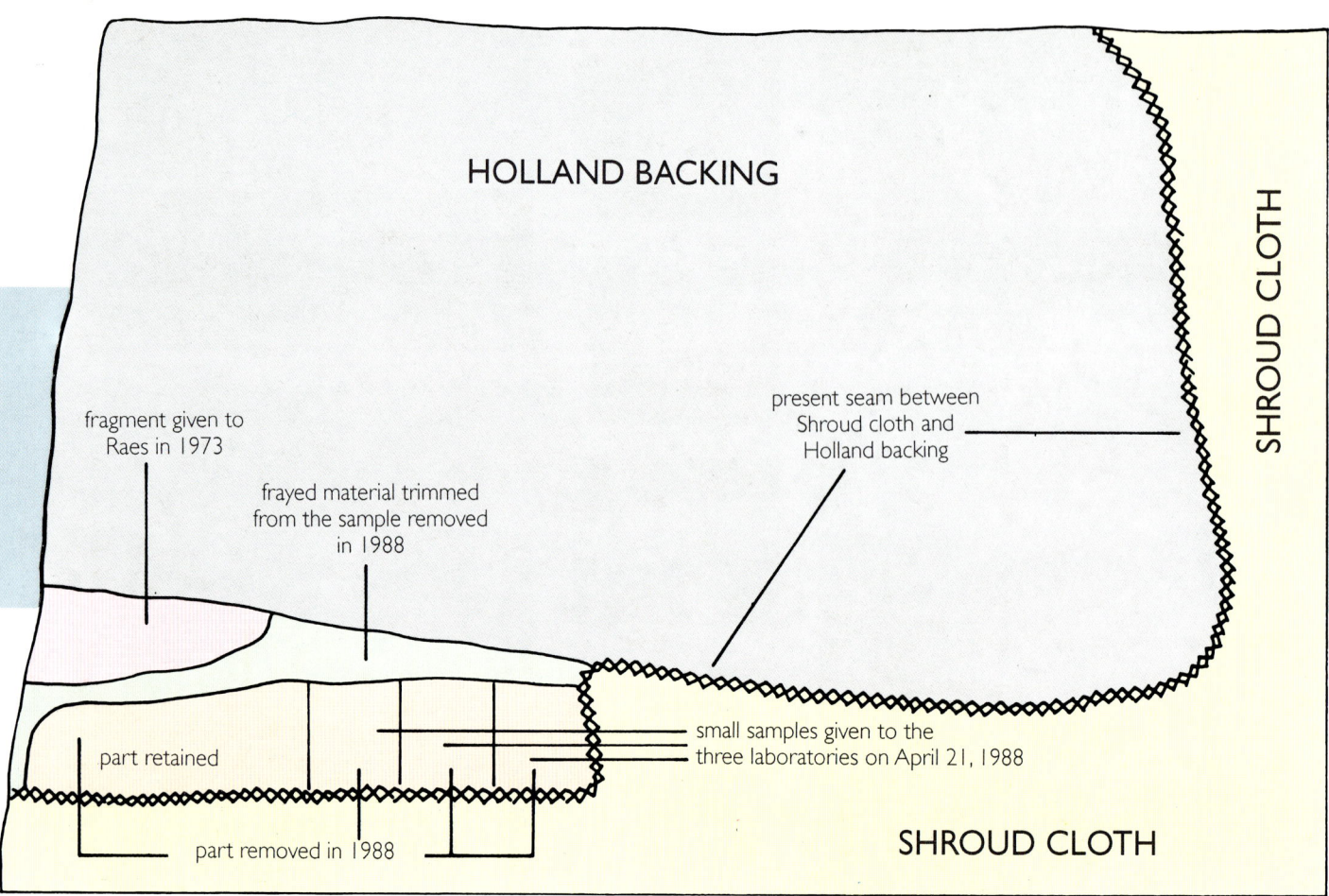

Diagram of the area of the Shroud (marked on the photo above) from which the samples of cloth were removed.

Zurich Polytechnik, Switzerland, was allocated little more than a square centimetre of the Shroud textile, for this to undergo dating by the Carbon 14 method. In addition, the laboratories received three small samples of anonymous textiles (in fact very easy to distinguish from that of the Shroud!). Dr Michael Tite of the British Museum, London, was appointed co-ordinator of the tests.

On October 13, 1988, six months after the samples had been taken, Cardinal Anastasio Ballestero, the then Archbishop of Turin and Pontifical Custodian of the Shroud, held a crowded press conference at which he read out a statement in which the three laboratories assigned a date between 1260 and 1390 for the cloth of the Shroud.

Afterwards, to the question put by a journalist: 'Why have you trusted science?' the Cardinal replied: *'Because science has asked for our trust. We all know very well the accusation science levels against the Church has always been that the Church fears science because science's 'truth' is superior to the Church's. Hence, to let science have its say seems to me to have been the Christian thing to do... Science has spoken; now science will have to evaluate its results... The Church is calm, has been and remains firm in insisting that the cult of the Holy Shroud will go on and that veneration for this sacred linen will remain one of the treasures of our Church... The Shroud has entered the liturgy of a Church; that shows how important and how efficacious it is. Science must speak as it finds; it is all too clear that what it has said is far from being the last word about this enigmatic sheet which evokes the face of Christ, and not the face alone, but the mystery of the Lord's passion and death, and probably his resurrection too.'*

(From *La Voce del Popolo*, November 6, 1988)

Many objections were raised against the behaviour of the three laboratories, especially as regards procedural correctness which did not conform to original undertakings.

Many people would like to see a re-run of the experiments, to take account of all observations made in the past, of recent scientific acquisitions, and to be generally integrated with all other spheres of research.

It is hoped that this may come about as a result of the next scientific congresses.

October 13, 1988. Card. Anastasio Ballestrero's press conference.

The Shroud of Turin and the Napkin of Oviedo

The Napkin of Oviedo (lit. sweat-cloth) is a rectangular piece of linen 821 x 526 mm. Since the 9th century it has been continuously and jealously guarded in the treasury of Oviedo Cathedral, Spain. It shows stains of varying tonality, most of them light brown.

According to an ancient tradition, it was placed over the face of Jesus (already wrapped in the Shroud) after he had been taken down from the cross.

From 1955 it was the object of particular study on the part of the late lamented sindonologist Mgr. Giulio RICCI, who observed the presence on the Napkin of certain characteristic stains (of serous blood) which he had also seen on the Face of the Man of the Shroud and which coincided with these both in measurement and in positioning.

First Professor Perluigi BAIMA BOLLONE of Turin and then Dr Carlo GOLDONI of Rome and a group of Spanish forensic doctors have established that some of the stains on the Napkin are certainly human blood belonging to blood group AB.

From October 29 – 31, 1994 the First International Congress on the Holy Napkin of Oviedo was held in the capital of the Asturias and reached *inter alia* the following conclusions:

- The Napkin of Oviedo seems to be a burial cloth which in all likelihood has been put over the face of an adult man of normal constitution.

- The Man of the Napkin had a beard, mustache and long hair gathered at the nape of the neck.

- The subject was a corpse. The mechanism forming the stains is incompatible with any possible respiratory movement (from *Linteum*, the review of the Spanish Sindological Centre, no. 12-13, December 1994, p. 24).

What about other shrouds?

There are many shrouds in Christendom: suffice it to scan the incomplete list printed in *Sindon N. S.*, 03/1991. None of them however can claim to be acheropita (i.e. not made by human hand), unlike the Shroud of Turin, and none is intended to look as if it were.

In centuries gone by there was a thriving industry in painted shrouds, possibly even in rare depictions of the body of the Redeemer, front and back. Yet all of them clearly show that they have been copied from an archetype, even when they do not bear an inscription indicating their provenance or the date when they were made. And all of them are attempts, often naive or clumsy, to produce an approximation to the Shroud of Turin, distinguished from them by the inimitable strangeness of the negative characteristic it alone, demonstrably and unequivocally, possesses.

Uninformed devotion sometimes ascribed extraordinary origins to certain copies of the Sacred Sheet. And so an object, the function of which was merely to call the Shroud to mind, came to be mistaken for the Shroud itself. This shows how wrong it is to say: 'There are many shrouds: so either they are all genuine, or none is.'

Below is a copy of the Shroud dated 1644, owned by the Capuchin Monastery in Turin, photographed and published here for the first time. Note the approximation of the *positive* and the unconvincing likeness that results from the photographic negative.

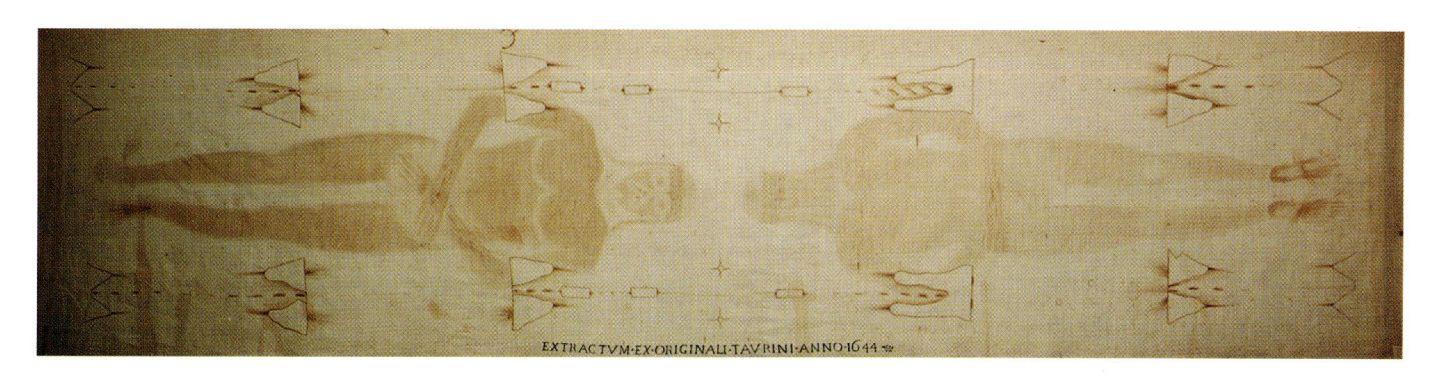

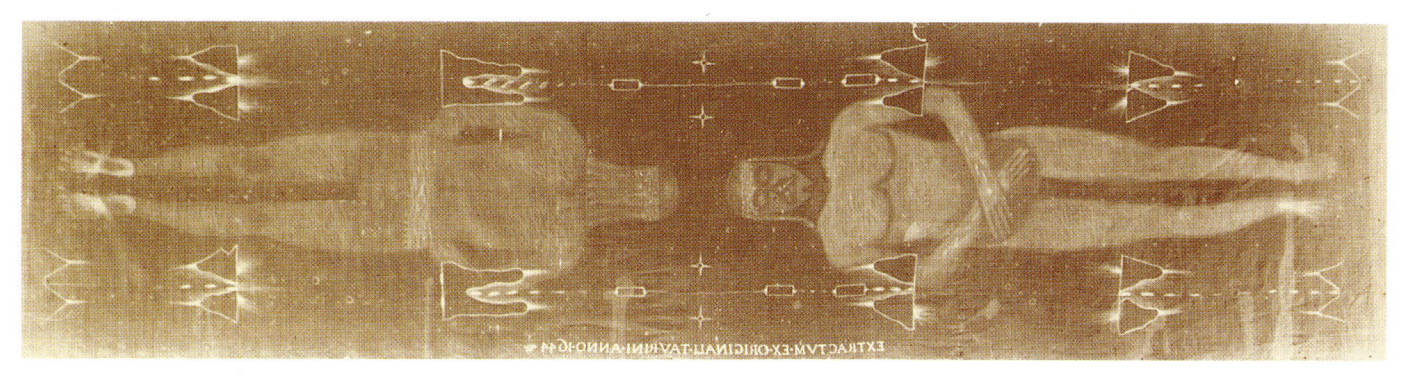

Another copy of the Holy Shroud, made in 1643, owned by Countess Alessandra Lovera di Maria.

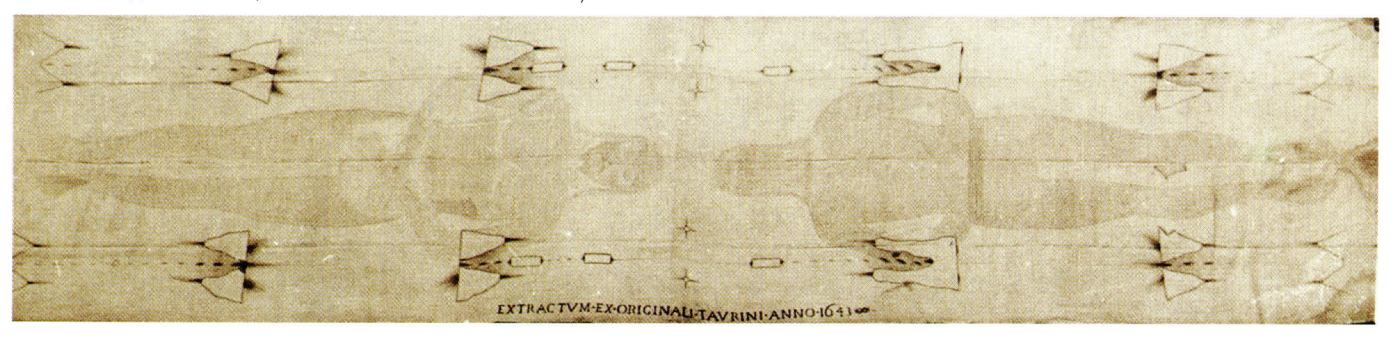

Can the Man of the Shroud be identified?

(Balance of Probabilities)

A number of scholars of critical disposition, intent on solving this mystery, have wondered whether the image imprinted on the Shroud might be that of Jesus Christ. Obviously this enquiry too, for it to be of scientific value, must be based exclusively on objective considerations. Here then is a study on the balance of probabilities, made by Professor Bruno Barberis of the University of Turin, reviving and completing studies by Yves Delage, Paul De Gail and Tino Zeuli. The method of research, while of absolute scientific rigour, is based on extremely simple considerations. The thesis is this:

If you throw a coin up in the air, the odds are two to one (1/2) it will land on the side you have chosen; if you throw a die up in the air, the odds against your getting the face of the die with your selected number on it are six to one (1/6). If you throw coin and die up at the same time, since the two events are independent of each other, the odds of your getting the preselected side of coin and face of die at the same time will be twelve to one (1/2 x 1/6 = 1/12).

Now let us examine the seven most significant characteristics common to Jesus of Nazareth (according to the Gospel narrative) and the Man of the Shroud, and see what the odds are against all these characteristics being found at the same time in the same man who had undergone the torment of crucifixion.

1. Both Jesus and the Man of the Shroud were wrapped in winding-sheets after death by crucifixion. Note that not many crucified men can have had a regular burial. (It was the most ignominious of punishments, reserved for slaves, brigands and murderers, and extended after death with contempt for the corpse): one chance in a hundred (1/100).

2. Both Jesus and the Man of the Shroud had a cap of thorns put on his head. No historical document mentions any such usage. Let us limit this very remote probability to one in five thousand (1/5000).

3. The *patibulum* weighed heavily on the shoulders of the Man of the Shroud as also on Jesus's. Only occasionally was the condemned man made to carry the horizontal beam of the cross to the place of execution: odds of two to one (1/2).

4. Same odds (1/2) on the way the hands and feet were fixed to the wood of the cross. They could be fastened with nails but a simpler and quicker method was to tie them on with ropes.

5. The Shroud displays a wound on the right side of the Man who was wrapped in it. John's Gospel (19:33-34) tells how in Jesus's case 'instead of their breaking his legs, one of the soldiers pierced his side with a lance, and immediately out came blood and water.' Odds perhaps of ten to one (1/10).

6. The Man of the Shroud had been wrapped in the sheet as soon as he was lowered from the cross; no washing or anointing of the corpse took place. It was the same with Jesus, since the Jewish Passover was about to begin, during which no manual labour could be performed: odds of twenty to one (1/20).

7. The Shroud bears the imprint of a man's corpse, but no traces of putrefaction. Hence it wrapped a human body for a brief period though long enough for an imprint to be formed on it. And did not the corpse of Jesus rest in the tomb for little more than thirty hours, from Friday evening until dawn on Sunday? This is an extraordinary case of agreement which we may rate at odds of five hundred to one (1/500).

From this analysis, Barberis then obtained the **aggregate probability**; this is given by the aggregate total of the individual probabilities considered, viz:

1/100 x 1/500 x 1/2 x 1/2 x 1/10 x 1/20 x 1/500 = 1/200,000,000,000

In line with the scholars preceding him, he was able to deduce that out of a hypothetical 200 billion victims of crucifixion **ONE ALONE** could have possessed the same identical characteristics common to Jesus and the Man of the Shroud' and the Gospel tells us what his name is: **JESUS CHRIST**, who suffered under Pontius Pilate, was crucified, died and was buried and who on the third day rose again from the dead.

ON THE MEDICAL EXAMINER'S TABLE

**Succinctly detailed examination of
six details of the exceptional, inexplicable human
form imprinted in negative on the Shroud
by a corpse that stayed wrapped in this sheet
long enough for the image to form but not more
than a certain number of hours,
since it has left no traces of putrefaction.**

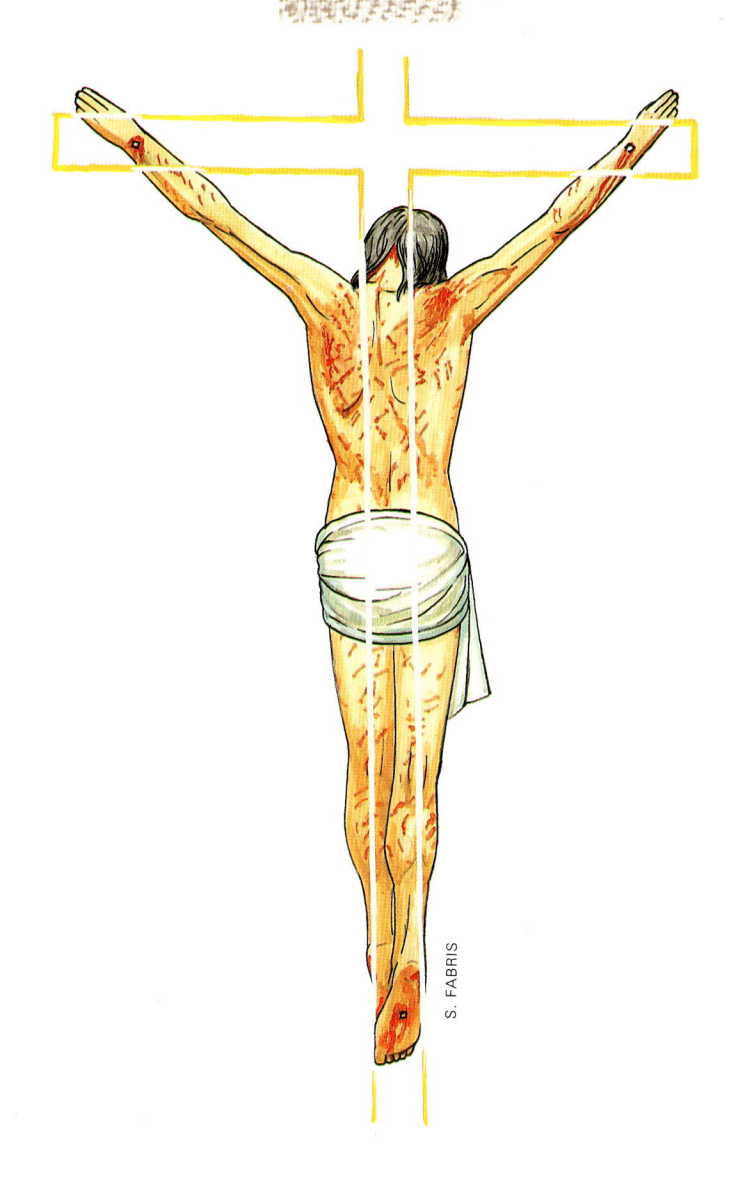

S. FABRIS

Imprint of the forehead
(PHOTOGRAPHIC POSITIVE)

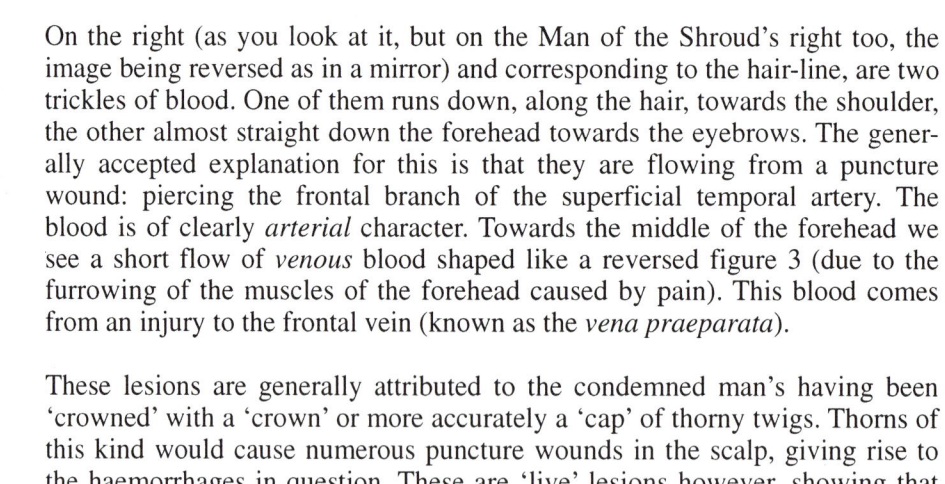

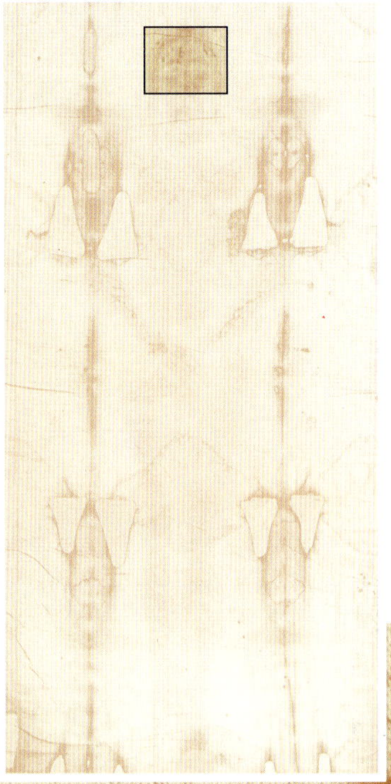

On the right (as you look at it, but on the Man of the Shroud's right too, the image being reversed as in a mirror) and corresponding to the hair-line, are two trickles of blood. One of them runs down, along the hair, towards the shoulder, the other almost straight down the forehead towards the eyebrows. The generally accepted explanation for this is that they are flowing from a puncture wound: piercing the frontal branch of the superficial temporal artery. The blood is of clearly *arterial* character. Towards the middle of the forehead we see a short flow of *venous* blood shaped like a reversed figure 3 (due to the furrowing of the muscles of the forehead caused by pain). This blood comes from an injury to the frontal vein (known as the *vena praeparata*).

These lesions are generally attributed to the condemned man's having been 'crowned' with a 'crown' or more accurately a 'cap' of thorny twigs. Thorns of this kind would cause numerous puncture wounds in the scalp, giving rise to the haemorrhages in question. These are 'live' lesions however, showing that the Man of the Shroud, when he was wounded by the thorns, was still alive.

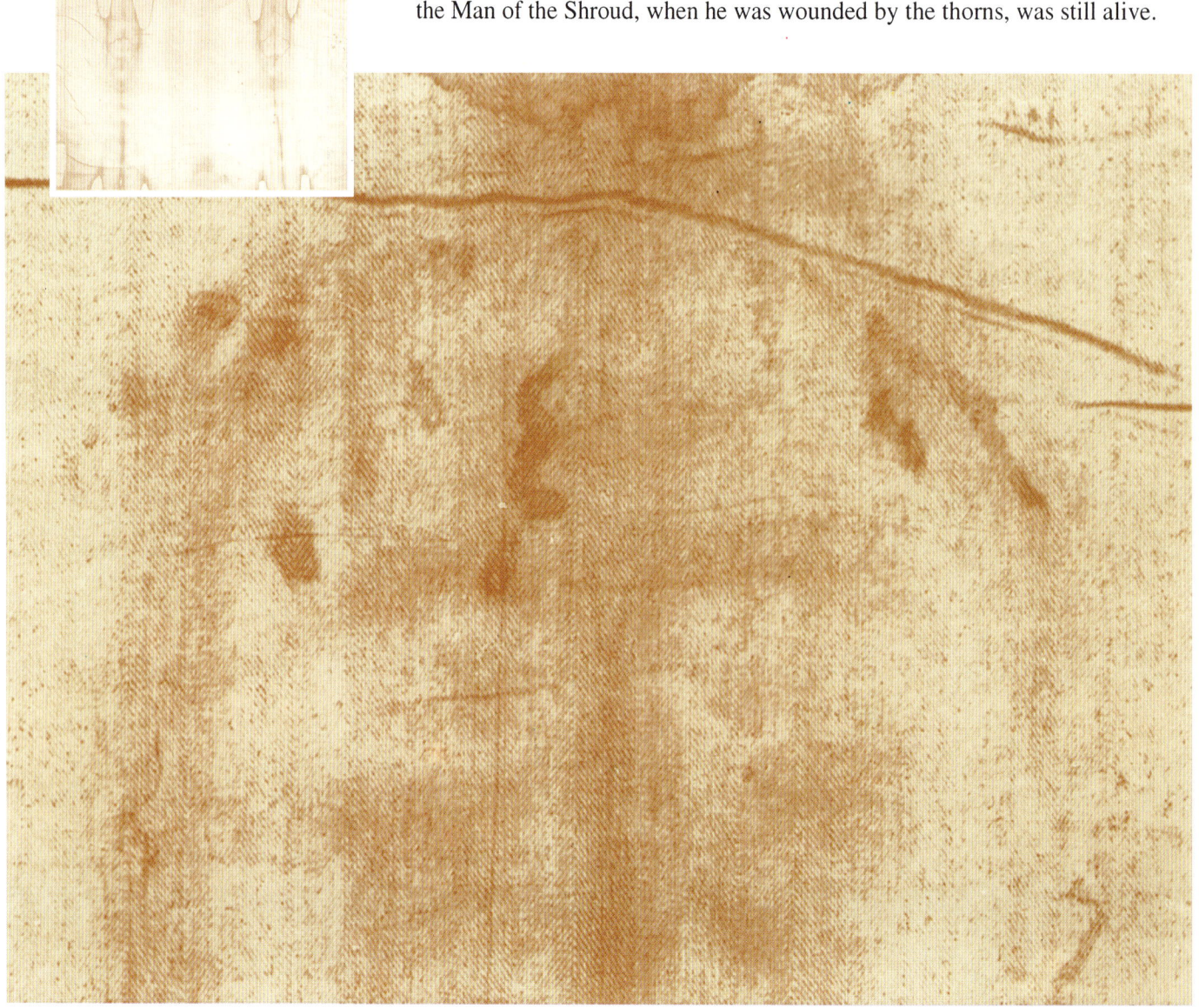

Imprint of the forehead
(PHOTOGRAPHIC NEGATIVE)

Photographic negative of same image shown in *photographic positive* on the opposite page.

Note:
the *inversion of light and shade*: light tonalities present in the *positive* have become dark in the *negative* and vice-versa;
the *mirror-like quality of the images*: what is seen on the right in the *positive*, is transferred to the left in the *negative*, and vice-versa.
Hence only the *negative* photograph of the part illustrated allows the face of the Man of the Shroud to be seen as it actually is.

The same explanation goes for the photographs reproduced on the following pages 62/63, 64/65, 66/67, 68/69 and 70/71.

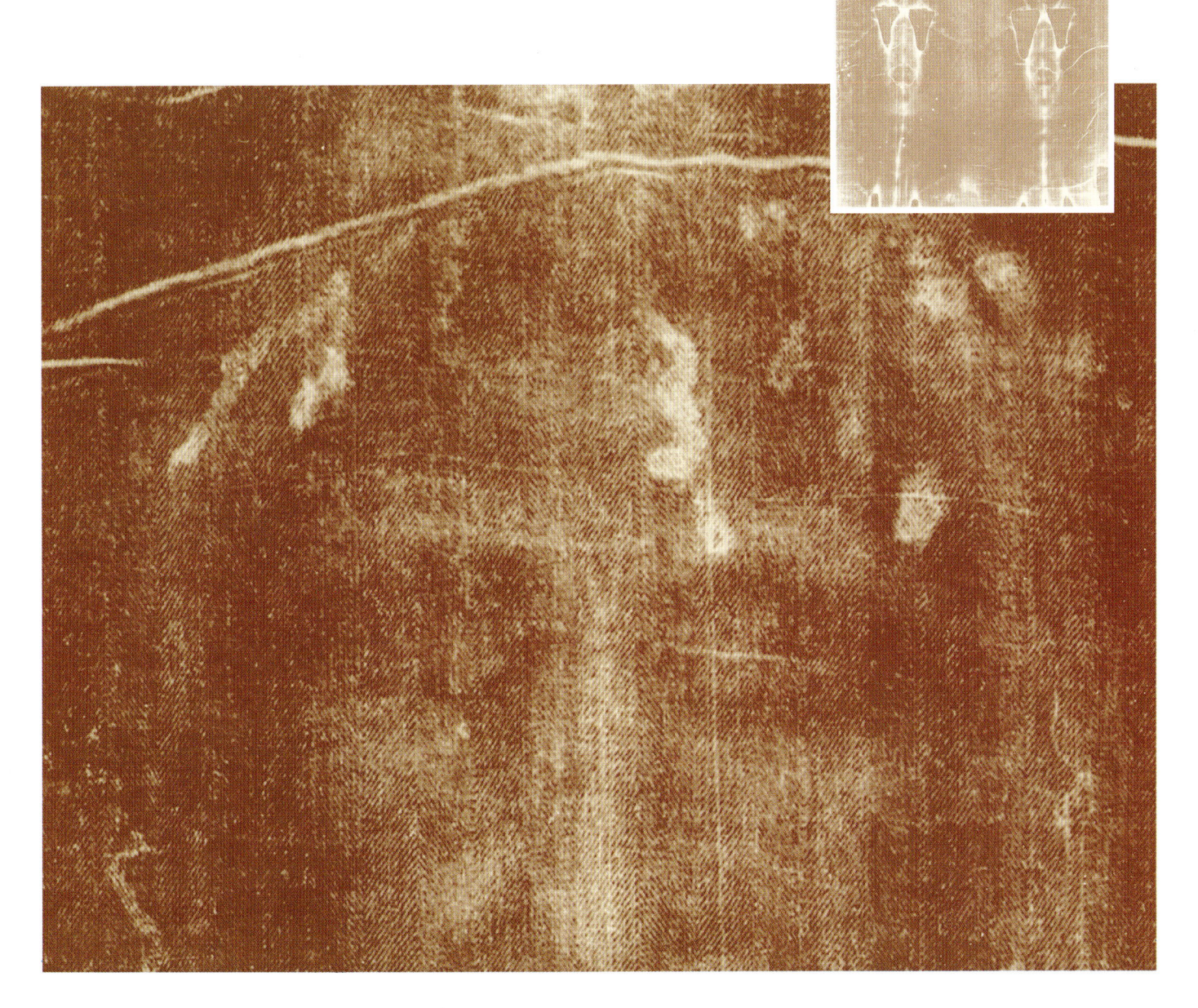

The wound in the chest
(PHOTOGRAPHIC POSITIVE)

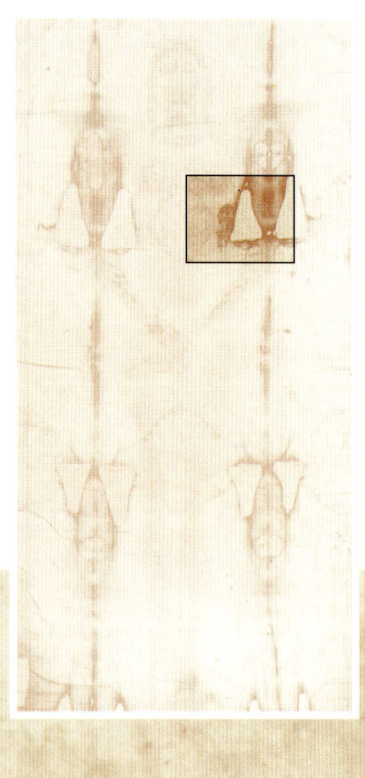

On the frontal section of the Shroud we see on the left hand side of the image (hence on the right hand side of the corpse) a wide blood-flow coming from a wound to the skin characterised by piercing and cutting. The bloodstain extends upwards at a width of at least 6 cm and runs downwards, dividing and meandering, for some 15 cm. This would correspond to the Roman soldier's lance thrust. Here we have a wound that has pierced the thoracic wall; which accounts for the copious flow of blood coming from it. The thrust has been delivered to a corpse, the nature of the fluid indicating that separation of the cellular and serous components has already taken place.

The most likely explanation for this is that during the Passion a haemothorax took place, i.e. that blood had leaked into the right pleural cavity. The lance thrust penetrating the thoracic wall after death, could not but release the sedimented blood with the cellular component which had sunk, to be followed by the serous component above it.

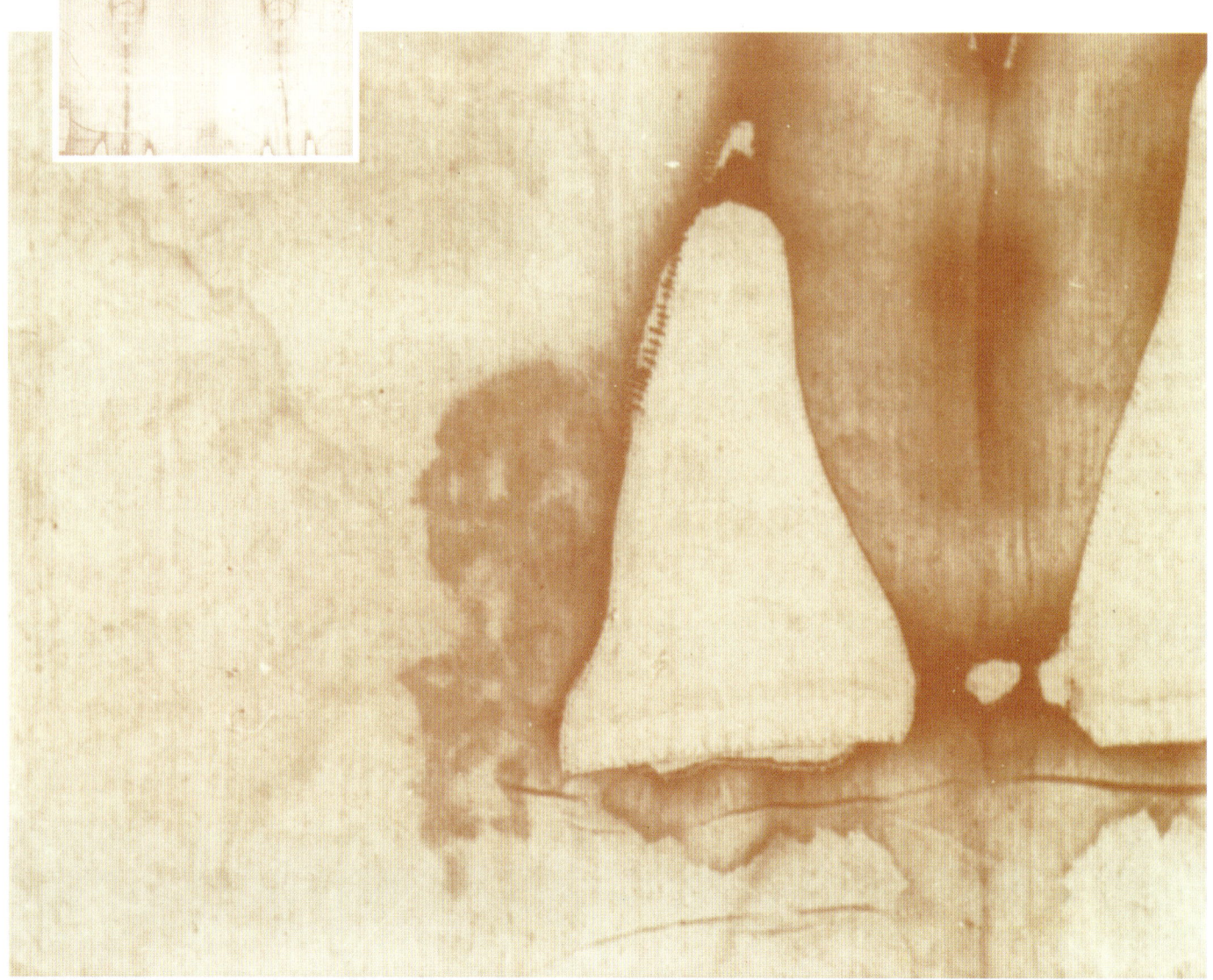

The wound in the chest
(PHOTOGRAPHIC NEGATIVE)

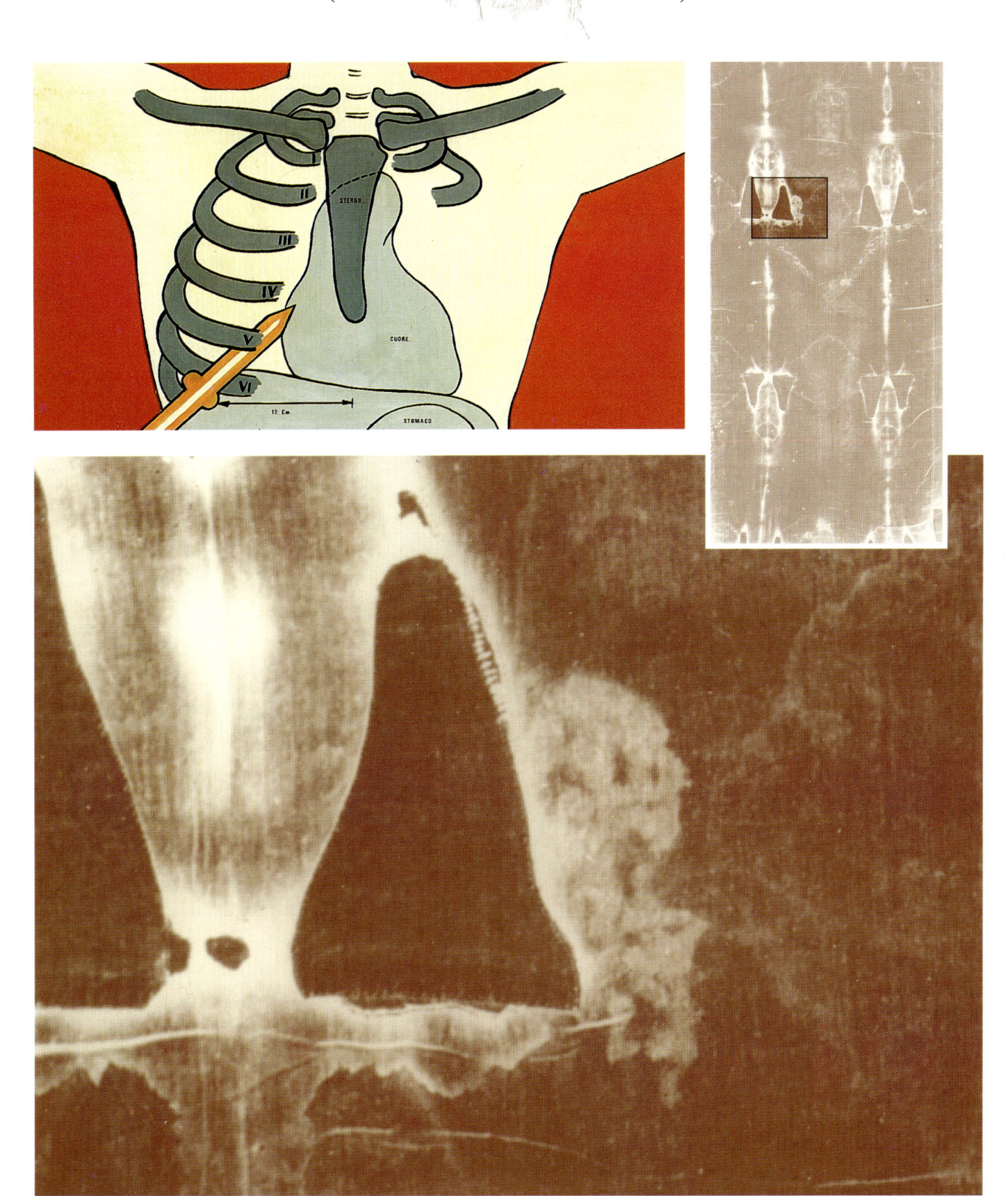

63

The forearms and the hands
(PHOTOGRAPHIC POSITIVE)

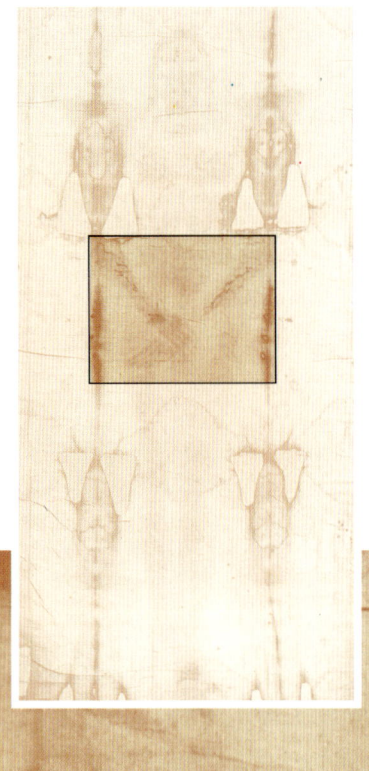

On the frontal imprint of the Shroud, a puncture wound may be seen, not actually in the palm (as iconographic tradition would have it) but corresponding to the 'space of Destot'. This is a natural gap between the bones, allowing easy insertion of a nail: hence the wound caused by nailing to the cross.

Driven through this space, the nail has damaged the median nerve (which is sensory and motor), provoking the contraction of the muscles with consequent closing of the thumb into the palm of the hand. For the thumb does not appear on the Shroud. Out of the question that a forger could have imagined and represented such a detail. The upper limbs of the corpse have been forced downwards for the hands to be crossed over the pubis.

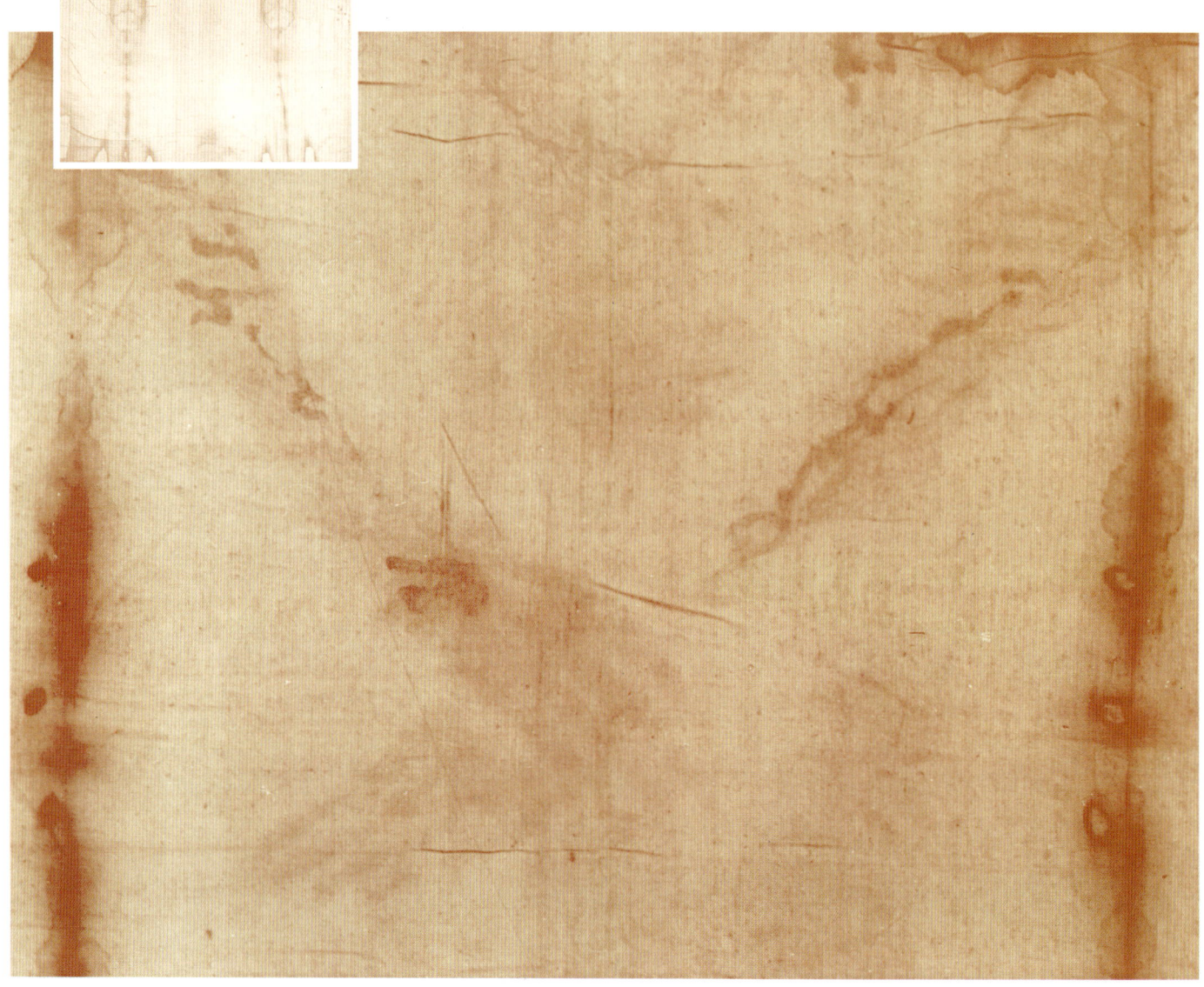

The forearms and the hands
(PHOTOGRAPHIC NEGATIVES)

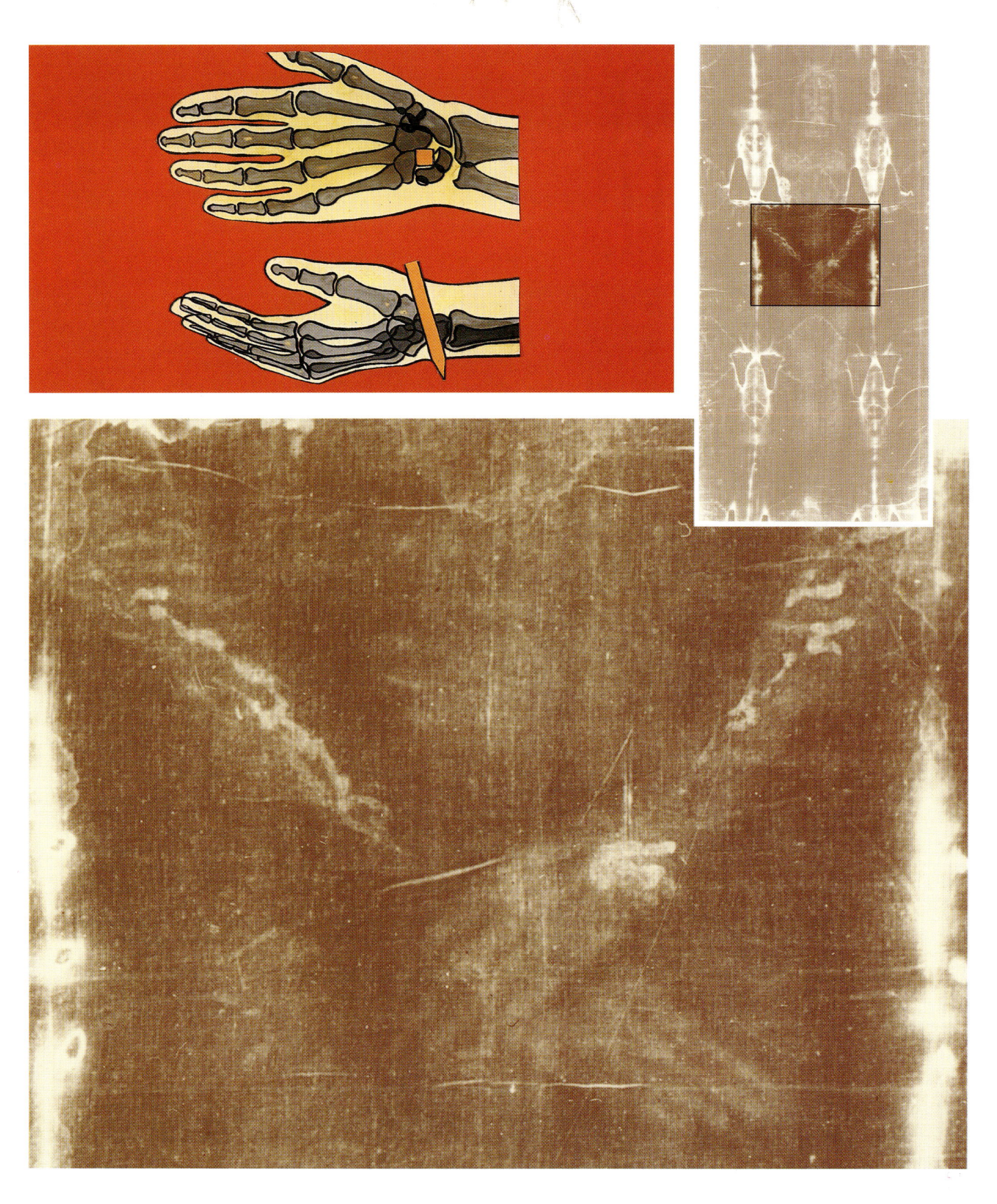

The nape and upper part of the back
(PHOTOGRAPHIC POSITIVE)

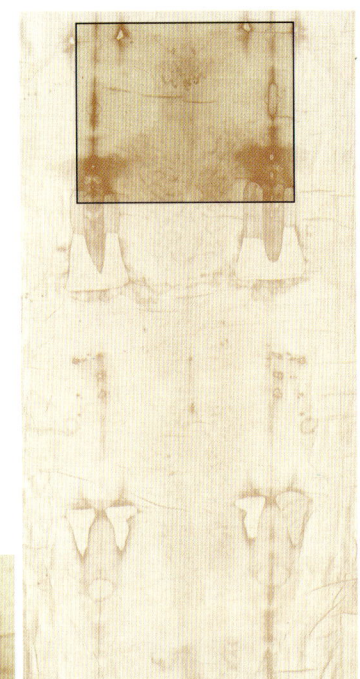

Haemorrhagic features occur on the nape of the neck, looking much the same as those on the forehead, though there are more of them: the deeply embedded thorns have probably damaged a branch of the occipital artery and the deeper veins of the posterior vertebral plexus.

The blood has arterio-venous characteristics (a mixture of arterial and venous blood) and has flowed through the hair and clotted in it.

The entire surface of the skin and particularly of the back shows lesions that remind us instinctively of the metal tips on Roman scourges.

Corresponding to the areas of the right shoulder and left shoulderablade are two areas of greater intensity in the image, which Barbet relates to the carrying of the horizontal member of the cross on the shoulders of the condemned man.

The thorns forming the 'caps' put on the Man of the Shroud's head were probably what botanists know as *Ziziphus spina Christi*, dramatically illustrated in the photo opposite.

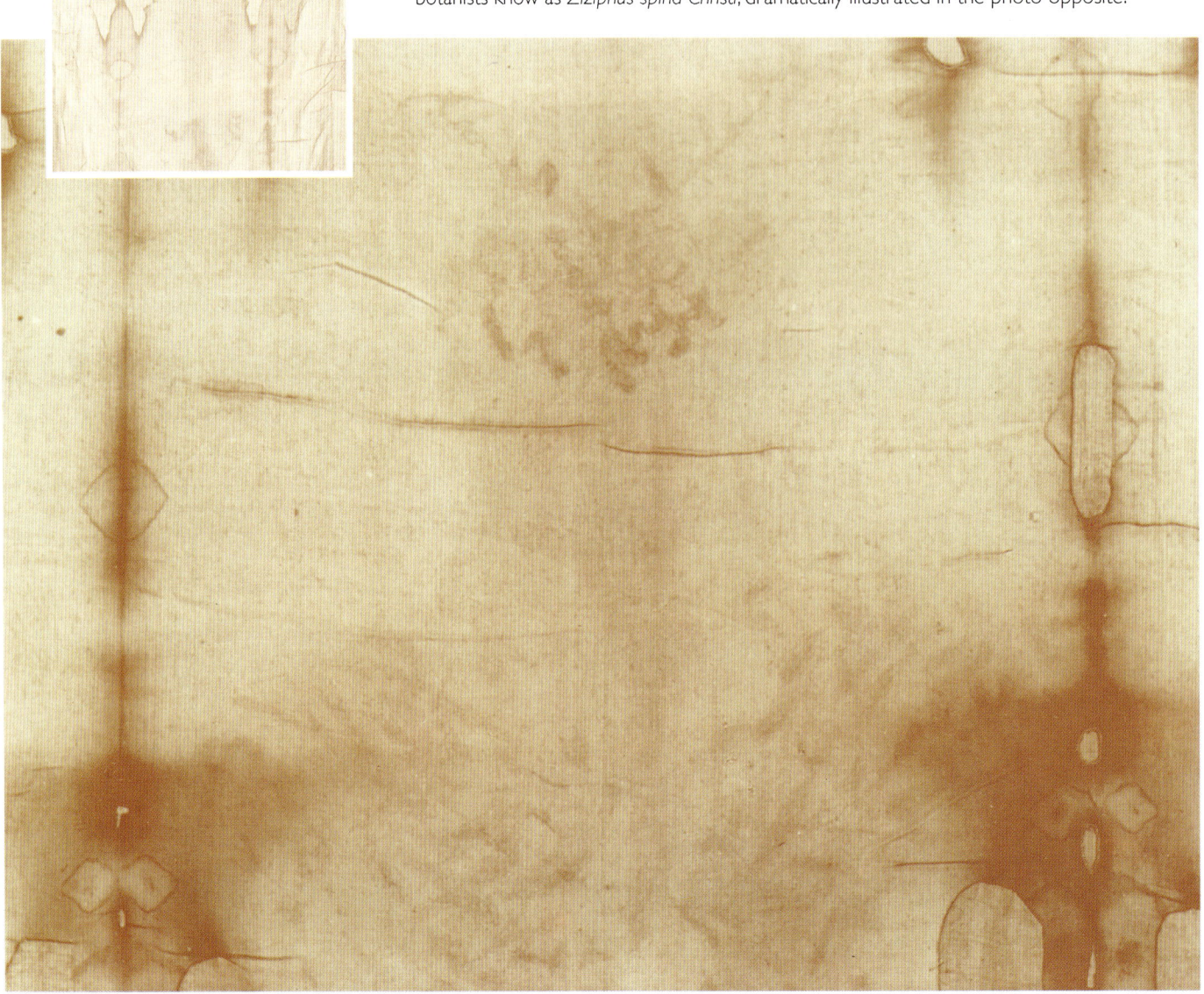

The nape and upper part of the back
(PHOTOGRAPHIC NEGATIVE)

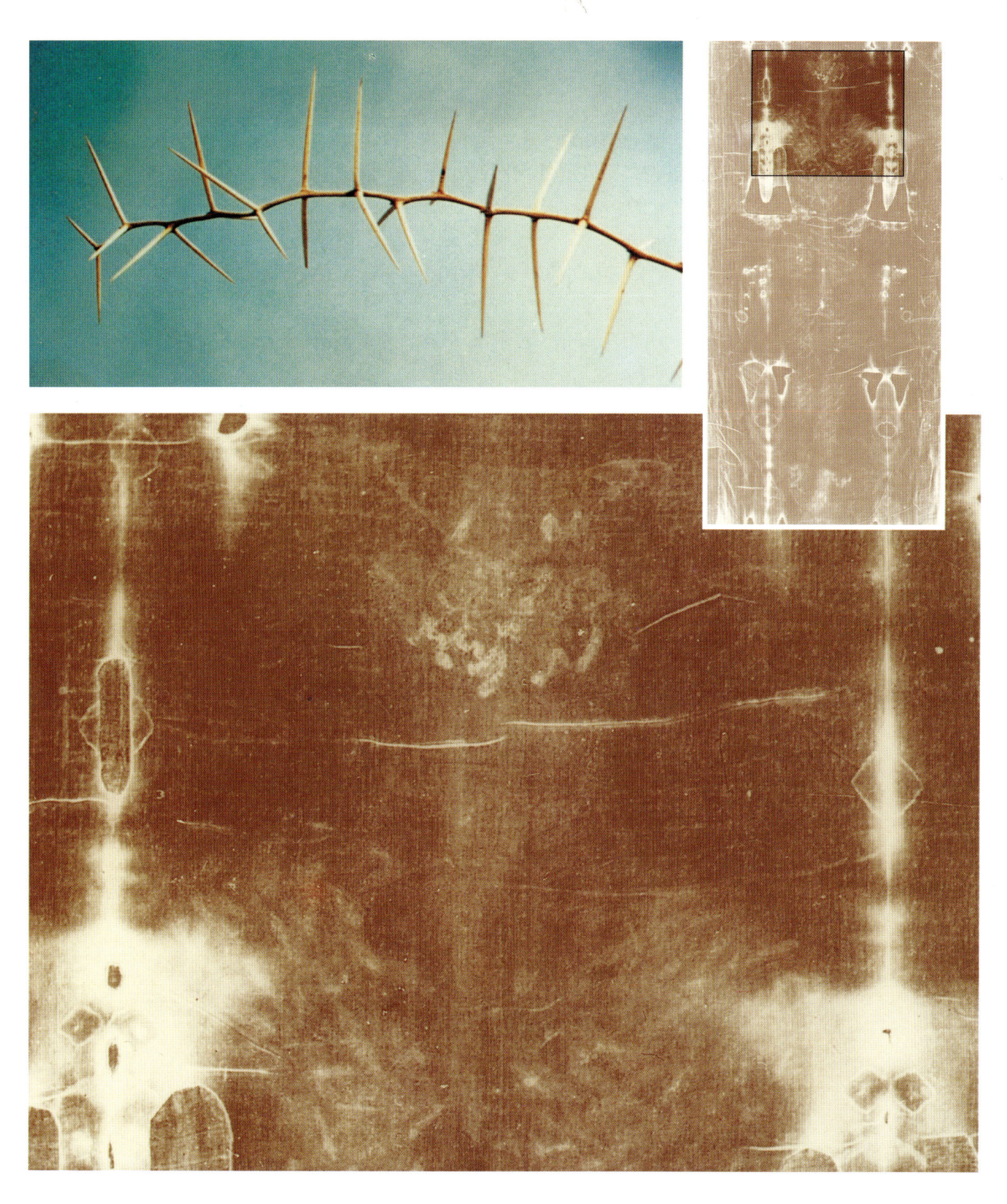

The blood-flow across the back
(PHOTOGRAPHIC POSITIVE)

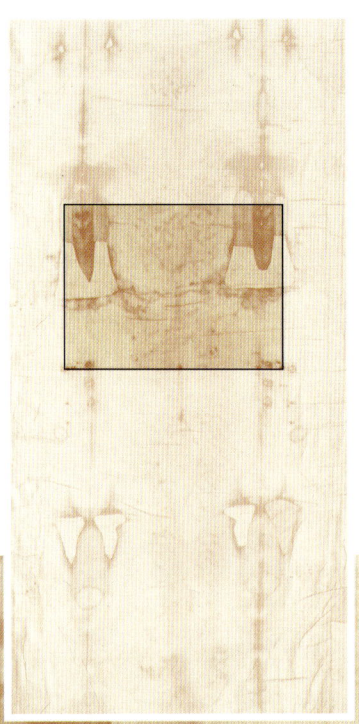

Blood-flow across the back caused by a second effusion of blood from the piercing-and-cutting wound to the chest. The blood first collected under the right elbow. From there, dividing into two channels, it crossed the entire lumbar region towards the left elbow, where it collected into another large stain.

The course of this *cadaveric* blood shows how the corpse was moved from one side to the other while being prepared for burial.

On the opposite page: a dramatic picture of Jesus being carried from the cross to the tomb in a winding-sheet, though certainly not one identifiable with the Shroud of Turin.
The painting is by A. Ciseri of Locarno.

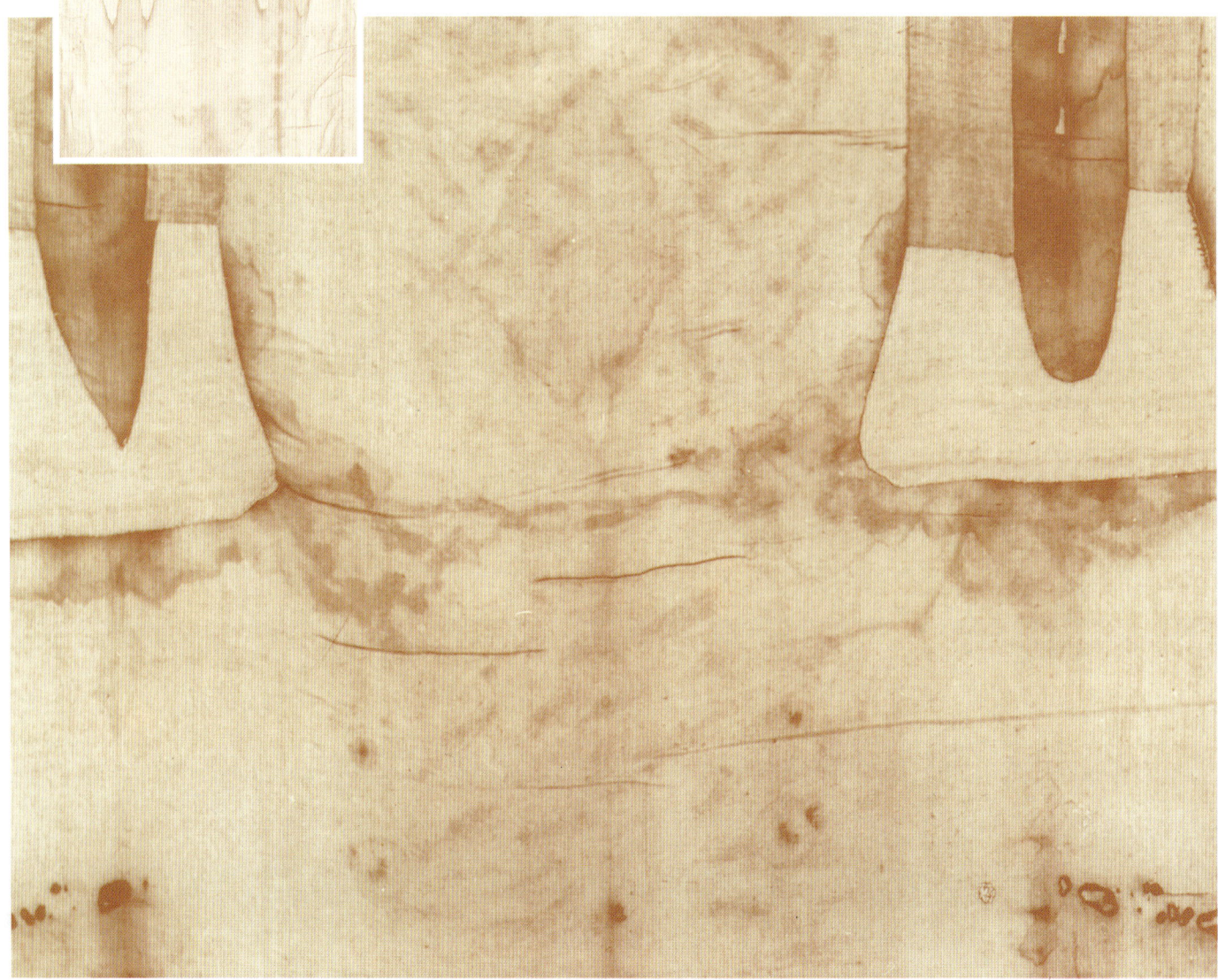

The blood-flow across the back
(PHOTOGRAPHIC NEGATIVE)

Imprint of the feet from behind
(PHOTOGRAPHIC POSITIVE)

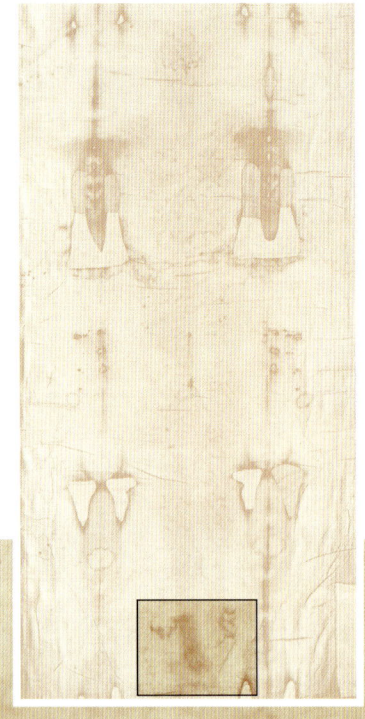

The right foot (left when looking at the image) has left a complete imprint, whereas only the heel and instep of the left foot can be seen, the imprint vanishing into the distance behind the right.

On the cross then the two feet were crossed: the left placed in front with its sole against the back of the right foot, which rested flat against the upright of the cross. (Note that in portraying the Crucified, artists often position the right foot over the left, when they do not show the feet actually apart!)

Beside the imprint of the right foot we can see the mirror-reflexion of a blood-flow, seeming to show how, at this point at least, the Shroud was drawn in sideways, being tied in some way we may suppose.

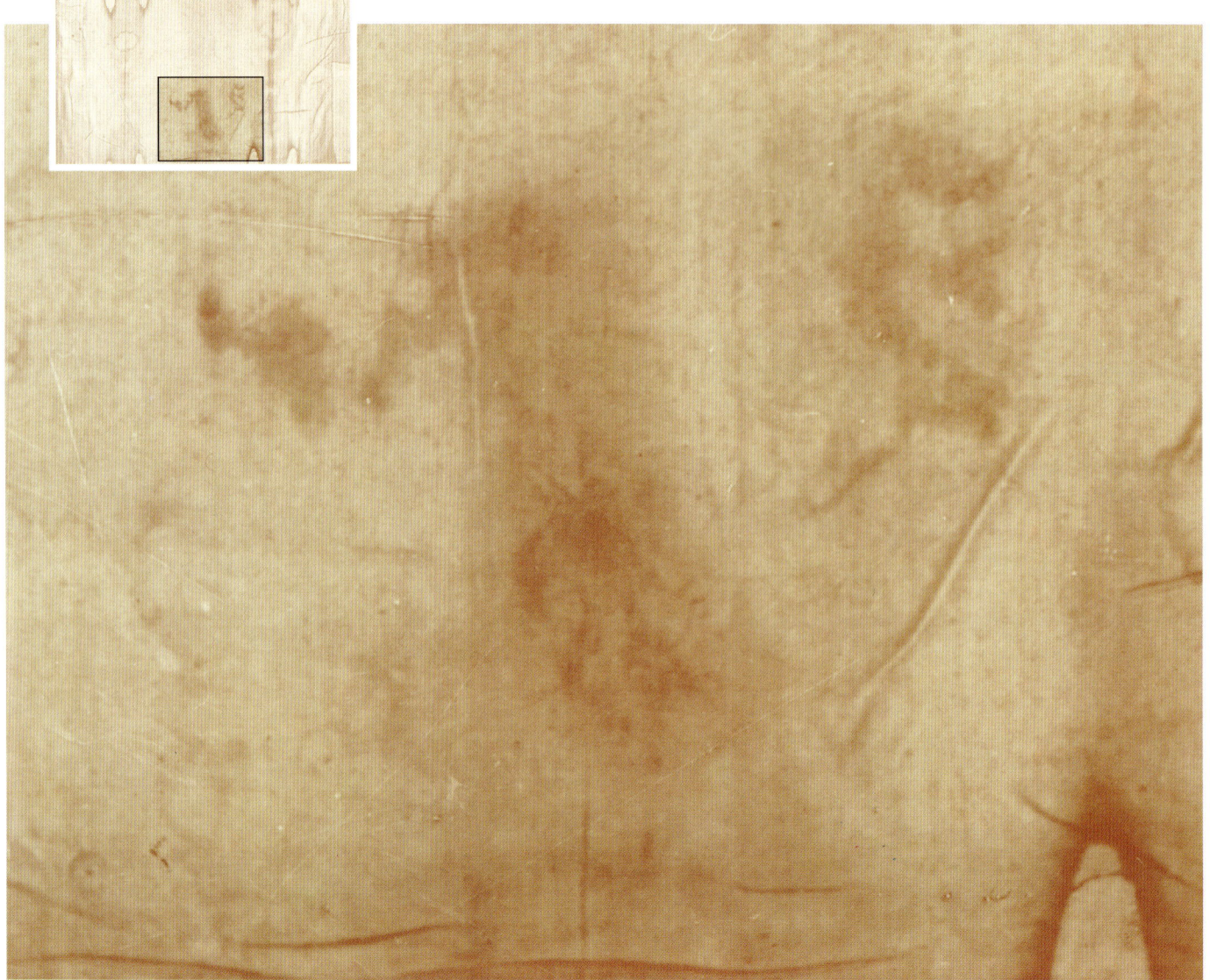

Imprint of the feet from behind
(PHOTOGRAPHIC NEGATIVE)

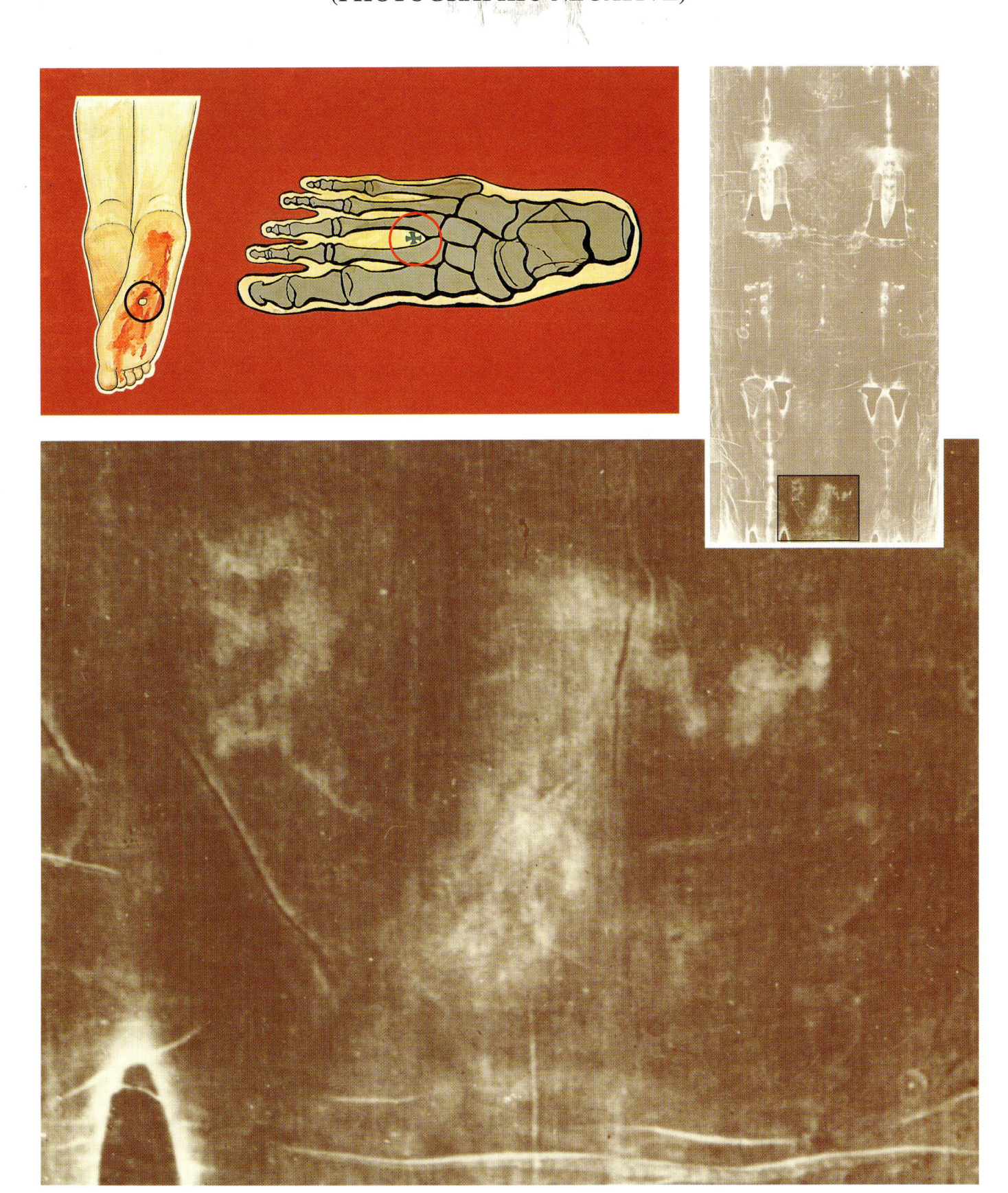

71

Conclusion

After examining these six photographs of details of the Shroud (three from the frontal section, three from the back) with commentary and captions for the most part drawn from studies by the medical doctors Pierre Barbet, Giuseppe Caselli and Pierluigi Baima Bollone, it remains for us to ask ourselves these questions:

■ Given the scientific certainty that this is not a painting, who, using what techniques many centuries ago, with extreme and impeccable realism, not making the slightest mistake, overlooking nothing, could have produced an image in *negative* when this concept only emerged in the first half of the 19th century with the discovery of photography?

■ Who could so perfectly have produced, so many centuries ago:
• Anatomical and pathological details of the human body?
• The various types of blood (arterial, venous, mixed and cadaveric)?
• The transfixing of the hands through the wrist-joint as anatomy requires if the body is to be supported, though this is in sharp contrast to centuries-old iconographical tradition?
• The retraction of the thumb due to injury to the median nerve?
• The wound on the left side of the chest and not on the right, an inversion which occurs only by substituting the *positive* for the *negative* image?

■ What brain could have worked out and positioned the dumb-bell shaped marks of flagellation, i.e. the way these are produced by the *flagrum*, and have indicated how these marks converge: *downwards* on the back, *crosswise* on the thighs, *upwards* on the calves, and all proceeding from one point, that is, from where the executioner must have been standing?

To make all the foregoing details consistent with a radiocarbon dating of the Shroud between 1260 and 1390 AD, one would have to postulate a cruel 'forger' in the Middle Ages who had deliberately subjected one of his contemporaries to Christ's entire martyrdom for the sole purpose of *impressing* this piece of linen on his corpse. But then, how could this 'forger' have got the image impressed on one side of the cloth only, when today, in the twentieth century, despite all scientific advances, how to produce a result of this kind is unknown? How could he have arranged for the presence on the cloth of grains of pollen coming from Palestine and Asia Minor, as well as from France and Italy? How could he, on the face of the Man of the Shroud, have represented details that only the recent invention of three-dimensional photography has been able to reveal, for instance the imprint of two coins, one on the right eye and the other on the arch of the left eyebrow.

Faced with such impressive convergence of circumstancial evidence supported by scientific proof, reason and coherence compel us to accept the message we receive from this Sheet, mysterious yet luminous as it is, and from the Man who was wrapped in it.

Yves Delage, a great French scientist and professor at the Sorbonne, not a believer, 'a free-thinker' as he liked to call himself, said in one of his reports to the Paris Academy of Sciences: 'If this is not the Christ, it must be some criminal or other. How are we to reconcile this latter possibility with the marvellous expression of nobility that this Image displays?' (from *Un non credente giudica la Sindone*, QUADERNI APERTI, no. 2, UMR, Trani, March 1983, p. 12).

JUDGMENTS AND DECISIONS OF THE ECCLESIASTICAL AUTHORITIES

S. FABRIS

PIUS XI (1922-1939)
Achille Ratti

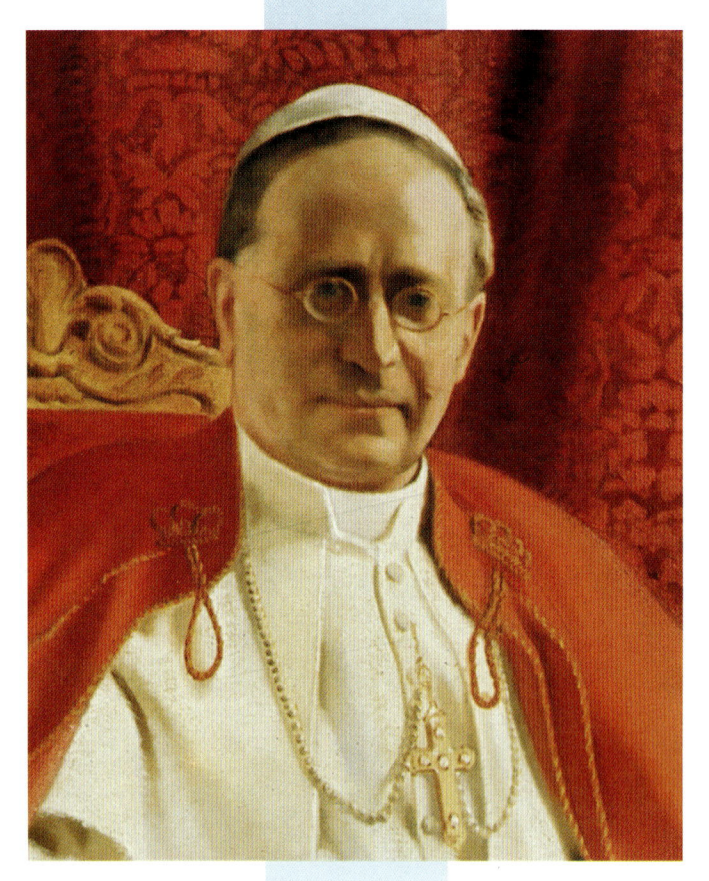

A historian on the throne of Peter, with a great devotion to the Holy Shroud.

He was particularly interested in research in the fields of science and the arts. In 1936 he founded the Pontifical Academy of Sciences. During his pontificate, two Expositions were held: in 1931 and 1933.

On March 21, 1934, when the official photographs of the Shroud taken by Giuseppe Enrie in 1931 were being presented to him, his comment was:
'These are worth more than all the study papers in the world!'

On September 5, 1936, while distributing pictures of the Holy Face on the Shroud to a group of young members of Catholic Action, he said:
'These are not pictures of the Blessed Virgin, it is true, but pictures that remind us of her as no other can. Since they are pictures of her Divine Son, and so, we can truly say, the most moving, loveliest, dearest ones that we can imagine. For they come from that still mysterious object (though certainly not made by human hand, for this has now been proved) which is the Holy Shroud of Turin' (*Osservatore Romano*, September 7-8, 1936).

PIUS XII (1939-1958)
Eugenio Pacelli

Admired for his deep spirituality, amazing culture and acute intelligence.

Pius XII's strictly ecclesiastical activity was in high relief especially in the dogmatic field where he tackled and resolved many important theological questions.

By nominating foreign cardinals he contributed to the internationalisation – in the non-European sense too – of the Sacred College of Cardinals.

At the close of the National Eucharistic Congress of 1953, he made a broadcast in which, among other things, he said:
'Turin, the City of the Most Holy Sacrament, guards as its precious treasure the Holy Shroud, which displays to our compunction and consolation, the image of the lifeless body and exhausted Divine Face of Jesus.'

JOHN XXIII (1958-1963)
Angelo Giuseppe Roncalli

A man of deep sensitivity, he acquired the nickname 'GOOD POPE JOHN'. He summoned the Second Vatican Council and was the first pope to travel beyond the walls of the Vatican (1962).

On February 16, 1959, in a fatherly address to the Groups of *Cultores Sanctae Sindonis* who had presented him with a collection of photographs of the Relic, Pope John repeated several times over and spelling out the words: '*Digitus Dei est hic!*' (The finger of God is in this).

PAUL VI (1963-1978)
Giovanni Battista Montini

A pope of lofty personality, he was the first pontiff to set foot on the American continent.
On June 4, 1967, in his homily to the pilgrims during the celebration of Mass in St Peter's, he said:
All artists have competed in rendering in colour and form the divine face of Jesus. But they are never satisfied. Perhaps the image of the Holy Shroud alone can tell us something about the mystery of this face which is at once human and divine.

On November 23, 1973, during the first televised Exposition, he gave a broadcast on the Holy Shroud:
'*The Face of Christ, represented on it, seems to us so real, so deep, so human, so divine, like no other image we have been able to admire and venerate... Whatever the historical and scientific judgement able scholars care to express about that astonishing and mysterious relic, we for our part cannot help but pray that it will avail in leading visitors not only to an absorbed and sensitive study of the outward and mortal lineaments of the marvellous face of the Saviour, but also in introducing them into a more penetrating vision of its inner, fascinating mystery*' (Sindon 19/1974, p.8).

JOHN PAUL II (from 1978)
Karol Wojtyla

A great Pope with an open, humane approach.
With the first 'Slav Pope' as he has three times described himself, the Church has taken on a new, universal dimension. In the history of the papacy, no pontiff has travelled so much and so far.

Having done homage to the Holy Shroud as a cardinal in 1978, he repeated his homage as Pontiff on April 13, 1980, at a brief private Exposition held during his visit to Turin.

On the latter occasion this is what he had to say:
'*It could not have befallen otherwise in the city that guards so unusual and mysterious a relic as the Holy Shroud, a most remarkable witness – if we accept many scientists' contentions – to Easter, to the passion, death and resurrection of our Lord. A witness mute yet astonishingly eloquent*' (*Osservatore Romano*, April 14-15, 1980, p.4).

Excerpt from an address given in Rome on April 20, 1980:
'…Then again, there is Turin Cathedral where the Holy Shroud has been kept for hundreds of years: that most radiant relic of Christ's Passion and resurrection…' (*Osservatore Romano*, April 21-22, 1980, p. 2).

CARDINAL GIOVANNI SALDARINI
Pontifical Custodian of the Holy Shroud

After the reflections of recent Pontiffs, this is what the present Archbishop of Turin, Cardinal Giovanni Saldarini, had to say during the liturgical Feast of the Shroud on May 4, 1990:

'*Two facts are incontrovertible as regards the Shroud. The first: on this sheet – and it is unique – there is imprinted the figure of a crucified man with marks of suffering and with wounds that tally in every particular with the description of the passion and death of Jesus as given in the Gospels. The second fact: from a scientific point of view, the Shroud constitutes a case so far unexplained. One may justifiably call it 'a prodigy of history' despite its vast heritage of research, even though this has not as yet been inter-disciplinary (as indeed we could wish). For the radio-carbon test itself, with all its limitations – and they are many – has only raised more questions than ever which a true science must now confront by consenting to re-examine every investigative procedure and every result. However (and let me say this clearly) the Faith does not depend on the Shroud's authenticity, nor has the Shroud ever been cited as proof of the truth of Christianity. This is why the believer can pursue research with a free, untroubled mind, whereas unbelievers might be put out of countenance, were they on the strength of historical and scientific investigations to find they have no choice but be convinced that what they are dealing with is the very winding-sheet in which Christ was wrapped.*'

Announcement on Expositions of the Shroud in the years 1998 and 2000

'With the full consent of the Holy Father John Paul II and in the context of the pastoral programme preparing for the Holy Year 2000, we are happy to announce that two Solemn Expositions will be held in Turin at Eastertide 1998 and 2000.

The reasons governing the choice of these dates are, as regards 1998, the five hundredth anniversary of the consecration of Turin Cathedral where the Holy Sheet is preserved, the Shroud so graphically reminding us of the mystery of our dear Redeemer's sufferings; and also the first centenary of the Exposition of 1898 when the first photograph was taken, this being the decisive factor in starting scientific research on the Shroud and thus distinguishing our own century from the others before it. The second Exposition in the Year of Jubilee is intended to offer a special opportunity for sanctifying the Jubilee by a penitential pilgrimage to this most moving sign of the Lord's passion. We hope that in both cases, as well as promising new departures in historical and scientific studies, the Exposition will be of very special value pastorally: for the eyes of the whole Church will be fastened on it.'

Turin, September 1995

✠ GIOVANNI CARD. SALDARINI
Archbishop of Turin
Custodian of the Holy Shroud

Motto of the 1998 Exposition:

ALL FLESH SHALL EXPERIENCE THE SALVATION OF OUR GOD

Official Logo of the Exposition

Statement on experiments concerning the Holy Shroud

'Certain organs of the press have been publishing news items concerning the Holy Shroud, on which the Pontifical Custodian feels it his duty to comment:

There are many news items increasingly circulating about experiments being conducted on samples of Shroud material with a view to checking the results of the analyses made by the Carbon-14 method in the summer of 1988. However legitimate the objective may be, and the Church recognises every scientist's right to carry out those forms of research he/she may regard as appropriate in his/her own scientific field, in the present case we must make it clear that:

a. no new material has been taken from the Holy Shroud since April 21, 1988, nor is it known to the Custody of the Shroud that any residual material then removed is in the hands of third parties;

b. if such material should exist, the Custodian puts on record that the Holy See has given no one permission to hold or make any use of it whatever, and requests the persons concerned to return it to the Holy See;

c. there being no degree of security governing possession of the materials on which the aforesaid experiments on the Shroud would have been conducted, the Holy See and the Custody declare themselves unable to ascribe any serious value to the results of such alleged experiments;

d. clearly this does not apply to research undertaken on material removed with the Custodian's explicit authorisation during the examinations of October 1978;

e. in an atmosphere of mutual trust with the scientific world, the Holy See and the Archbishop of Turin invite scientists to be patient until the time comes for implementing a clear and concerted programme of research.

Turin, September 1995

✠ GIOVANNI CARD. SALDARINI
Archbishop of Turin
Custodian of the Holy Shroud

During the 1998 Exposition, the Third International Congress of Sindonic Studies, organised by the International Centre for Sindonic Studies of Turin, will be held in Turin between 5th and 7th June. The Congress will discuss the theme: The Shroud and Science, an assessment and programmes for the future as we approach the threshold of the Third Millennium.

The Confraternity of the Most Holy Shroud
The International Centre of Sindonology of Turin

The Confraternity of the Most Holy Shroud and the Blessed Virgin of Graces was founded in 1598, barely 20 years after the Shroud's arrival in Turin.

As well as spreading knowledge of and devotion to the Shroud, the Confraternity devoted itself to helping the mentally sick and poor and needy young women, as also to the religious instruction of certain categories of the people of Turin.

In 1729 the Confraternity built the *Ospedale de'pazzerelli* (lunatic asylum) and a few years later the present Church of the Most Holy Shroud.

Within the Confraternity in 1937 a guild was set up called the *Cultores Sanctæ Sindonis*, which in 1959 by decree of Cardinal Maurilio Fossati, Archbishop of Turin, was transformed into the *Centro Internazionale di Sindonologia* (International Centre of Sindonology of Turin).

The Centre, with its premises at Via S. Domenico, 28 – 10122 TURIN (tel. & Fax 011-43 65 832), is divided into Delegations and Groups.

In accordance with its statute:
- it organises and promotes national and international displays, meetings and congresses;
- publishes the Sindon booklets, the official organ for reports, reviews and articles by Italian and foreign scholars on their investigations and historical, exegetical, medical, chemical and physical research directly or indirectly concerned with the Holy Shroud;
- monitors literary and iconographical work to ensure nothing is published that could in any way damage reverence for or devotion to the Shroud.

We should like to point out that study centres and pastoral sindological centres are now to be found in every continent.

Above: the high altar of the Church of the Most Holy Shroud with above it a life-size copy of the Shroud.

Left: the facade of the church, modelled on that of the Sainte-Chapelle at Chambéry.

The Museum of the Shroud

In the courtyard of our premises at 28, Via San Domenico, Turin, is the only museum of its kind in the world: The **Museum of the Shroud** (*Museo della Sindone*).

It houses rare relics marking the Shroud's history and the results of research carried out on it.

To the Museum are attached a substantial sindonological library in various languages, a rich iconographical collection and an impressive 'Historical Archive'. At present, entrance is free on the days and at the times shown on the doorplate reproduced below (Monday-Friday 15.00-18.00).

On October 9, 1995, on the occasion of a 'Concert devoted to the Shroud' in the Church of the Most Holy Shroud next door, the Museum was visited by the Italian Head of State, Oscar Luigi Scalfaro.

Castelnuovo Don Bosco (Asti)